Revised and Expanded Third Edition

MOTORCYCLE YOGA

A Pilgrimage through Ancient India
1981–2000

Patita Pavana dasa Adhikary

(Miles Davis)

Bookwrights Press
Charlottesville, VA

Motorcycle Yoga
Revised and Expanded Third Edition

Copyright © 2024 by Miles Davis (Patita Pavana Dasa)
All Rights Reserved.

No part of this publication may be reproduced in any form without prior permission from the author or publisher.

Published by

Bookwrights Press
Charlottesville, VA
publisher@bookwrightspress.com
www.bookwrightspress.com

ISBN: 978-1-880404-61-4

Cover and text designed by Mayapriya devi dasi
Text photos by the author

Dedication

To Shrila Prabhupada and every servant of His Divine grace

London, 1973

Prabhupada ordered Patita Pavana to read from his Krishna book, the Supreme Personality of Godhead, at a yagna, ISKCON Press, Boston, 1969

The author in India in the mid-seventies

Contents

Jai Hind	vi
Preface: The Ride of a Lifetime	vii
Introduction: Moto-Biography of a *Yogi*	ix
1. Riding Bombay 1981: "The Journey of a Thousand Miles Begins with First Gear"	1
2. Kipling's India: "A Bubble Burst In Time"	7
3. The Road of Bhera Ghat: "Rolling with the River"	21
4. Around Damoh: "...Of Dogs and Men and Demigods"	28
5. The Devi Road: "The Eightfold Path on Highway Seven"	71
6. Discovering Parashurama Kunda: "The *Avatara* and the Axe"	87
7. The Ride to Rama Giri: "Lord Rama's Weapons"	97
8. At a Spotlight in Nagpur: "A Moment to Reflect"	106
Epilogue: Yoga Is	131

Jai Hind

She who is washed by three great oceans,
The Breath of God Her wind,
Protected by Himalayan peaks,
She is the Land called Hind.
This place on Earth is sacred,
Sadhus, saints and sannyasins,
Bow in the dust of Mother India,
To find the heart of Hind.
In this land of Bharata-bhumi,
Where every wish is pinned,
May you encounter gentle souls,
The shining jewels of Hind.
May inner wisdom ever guide you,
Far above the smoke and din,
And may you learn the lessons,
Locked in the lore of Hind.
May you seek the brotherhood of Man,
Each wayfarer your next of kin,
And may you share the dignity,
Of the *dharma* that is Hind.
And find your place in the Universal,
Balance of yang and yin,
Poised between Shiva and Shakti,
Who bless Their land called Hind.
May you tread the path of piety,
Rejecting vice and sin,
May goodness shine from within you,
Like the sages who walk Hind.
May victory ride ever beside you,
Like Arjuna who battled to win,
May you conquer each soldier of evil,
To find Kurukshetra in Hind.
In this land of Lords Rama and Krishna,
Where *devas* come marching in,
May you find within your heartbeat,
The bliss that flows from Hind!

—Miles Davis

Preface
The Ride of a Lifetime

MOTORCYCLE YOGA IS A TRUE CHRONICLE of one man's journey on two wheels into the heart of India and into the inner sanctum of the spirit. Here in these pages and with the tapestry of my country's diverse landscape as a backdrop, the reader relives with the author his motorcycle adventures and misadventures, enjoying the pulse of the ride as a fellow traveler accompanying the journey. Seated either upon a legendary Royal Enfield Bullet, or upon a Indo-Czech Jawa or even on a humble Vespa; we journey with Miles Davis to *ashrams* of *yogis* and Jain munis, to horrifying days in an Indian jail on false charges, to the center of deadly riots, to a roadside garbage heap where the author finds himself for days too weak from malaria to move.

And as the reader rides along he quickly forms a spiritual partnership in the ecstatic quest for truth and light that can only be found beyond the curtain of illusion. It is the search for the Soul of all souls that remains the driving force of Motorcycle *Yoga*. Riding on through crowded bazaars, to caves, to riverside hermitages, to forest retreats, to hill temples to the waters of cool rivers we discover the best and worst in the nature of man. Therefore it is understandable if the bittersweet humor of a survivor sometimes surfaces from the mix of adventures that has created *Motorcycle Yoga*, for in the game of survival the naked truth alone can win.

Motorcycle Yoga is also a treasure of esoteric knowledge freely shared, a rare journey into the singular neo-art form of transcendental moto-meditation. This is one of those books that once you pick it up, it is hard put down. No one ever guaranteed that The Ride and the adventure of the soul would always be an easy one, and this is the element that makes Motorcycle *Yoga* all the more compelling.

I have enjoyed a few memorable two wheeling adventures with Miles Davis or Pavan (meaning "wind") as we call him, riding out together to secret and little known central Indian holy spots like the Ram Tek Hill or the temple village Kundina. Because I enjoy two-wheel adventure, Motorcycle *Yoga* was for me the ride of a lifetime, a ride into little known and less understood regions of the world and of consciousness.

Anukaran Singh
Co-founder: Nagpur Royal Enfield Bullet Club
Nagpur, India

Introduction
Moto-Biography of a *Yogi*

Motorcycle Yoga is the story of *tirtha yatra*, of visiting India's holy places. From the Himalayas to Kanya Kumari, the vast sub-continent has four holy abodes *(chatura-dhama)*, seven holy cities *(sapta-puri)*, seven holy rivers *(sapta-puri)*, twelve main temples of Lord Shiva *(dwadasha jyotira-linga)*, five great holy places *(mahastans)*, fifty-one shrines of the Mother Goddess *(shakti pithas)*, as well as many holy places dedicated to the sons of Shiva and Parvati, Ganesh *(ashta-Vinayaka tirtha)* and Kartikeya *(shad-Skanda kshetra)*. Along almost all woodsy paths you'll find temples to Hanuman.

Even before I acquired the Royal Enfield 350cc in 1999, I had been blessed to visit a huge number of them, and thousands of other sacred spots along the way. After getting the bike, I discovered that the experience of *tirtha-yatra* becomes magnified on a slow two-wheeling journey through the back roads of Central India—and a few of those rides are the focus of *Motorcycle Yoga*. While moving on two wheels alone in the middle of nowhere, the destination becomes more meaningful. Getting there and back on a motorcycle is a total experience; something that cars, buses and trains just cannot offer.

Shrila Prabhupada must have supported my *tirtha-yatra* fantasies, because he wrote to me (referring to me by the other name he gave me):

My dear Patita Uddharana dasa,
Please accept my blessings.
I am in due receipt of your letter dated March 17th, 1975 and have noted the contents. Thank you for your articles. They are very nicely writ-

ten. They (the newspaper) have given us a good amount of space. That means that we can present our philosophy in detail and they will read it. Regarding that man Mr. Shah, you can ask him what is the best season for going to Dvaraka. Then I shall arrange for going there. I have never been there yet.

I hope this meets you in good health.
Your ever well-wisher,
A.C. Bhaktivedanta Swami

Sixteen years back, by the will of Lord Krishna, who guides the wanderings of all living entities, I shifted gears to Eastern Europe, to the Rila Mountains of Bulgaria, where the search for *punya bhumis* and *tirthas* continues. Along with my beloved companion and *dharma-patni*, Abhaya Mudra Dasi, we have together found remnants of Vedic civilization and culture throughout this great land of Bulgaria, from its border with Macedonia all the way to Black Sea beaches. We have stood on the shore of the river of the Danavas, the Danube, and explored the underworld cave of Orpheus, who is none other than Narada Muni in local lore. We swam in the lake where a great demon, much like those described in *Mahabharata* and *Ramayana,* once bedeviled the citizens, Together we have been to the temple of Jupiter (Brihaspati) at old Theopolis (God's city), now called Obzor.

We have seen ancient abandoned Shiva temples, and watched from the hot springs in the Kozhuh Volcano as the ancient Vedic town of Heraclea Sintica literally emerged from the volcano's walls. We have seen the solid gold *jileri* of Panagyurishte, the emblem of the Goddess upon which once stood a Shiva *linga*. We have been up into the Pirin Mountain where ancient Thracians worshiped Indra, the lord of rain, along with his sister Echo. We have been to many Thracian mounds that were once places of pre-Christian worship.

We visited the *samadhi* of Peter Deunov, who introduced Vedic ideology in Bulgaria in the 1940s; and the *ashrams* of blind lady prophets *Baba* Vanga and *Baba* Stoyna. We have been to the forests where Christian mystics, the Bogomils, penanced long ago. We attended the *kukeri* festivities, a more modern interpretation of Makara Sankranti, where our daughters Yamini and Jaya Radhe joined the folk dance of celebration.

We have been to the cave of Saint Ivan of the Rilas, a genuine Christian saint, unlike mythological personalities manufactured by monks to lead people away from "paganism." We have seen the Vedic symbols carved on ancient churches that were long ago converted from centers of Sun god worship to Christian halls of prayer. We have seen 1,000-year old abandoned churches of various saints that were once temples of various demigods. Along the way, the church fathers conventiently changed the demigods into saints, which is the subject of Abhaya Mudra Dasi's book *Modern Saints, Ancient Deities*. Thus, in the company of my family, another ride and another chapter into Vedic culture and the coming Golden Age continues.

༄༅

Shrila Prabhupada writes in Chapter Seven of *Teachings of Lord Chaitanya*, "In Anandaraṇya there is the form of Vishnu, and in Mayapur, the birthplace of Lord Chaitanya, there is the form of Hari. Many other forms are also situated in various places on the earth. Not only in this universe, but in all other universes as well the forms of Krishna are distributed everywhere. It is indicated that this earth is divided into seven islands, which are the seven continents, and it is understood that on each and every island there are similar forms, but at the present moment these are found only in India. Although from Vedic literatures we can understand that there are forms in other parts of the world, at present there is no information of their location.

"The different forms of Krishna are distributed throughout the universe to give pleasure to the devotees. It is not that devotees are born only in India. There are devotees in all parts of the world, but they have simply forgotten their identity. These forms incarnate not only to give pleasure to the devotee, but to reestablish devotional service and perform other activities which vitally concern the Supreme Personality of Godhead. Some of these forms are incarnations mentioned in the scriptures."

Vyasadeva's great history of India, *Mahabharata*, likewise explains that Vedic culture was once spread throughout the world. India is known as Bharata, named for the royal son of King Rishabhadeva. Since the influence of Vedic culture broke the boundaries of the great seas that surround India, *sanatana dharma* spread far beyond the Sindh and Brahmaputra Rivers. This is the actual meaning of "Mahabharata," or "the greater India." Since Prabhupada wrote the prophetic words that are quoted above over half a century back, Vedic deities, along with evidence of the world's oldest *dharma*, are mystically appearing in the Near East, in Africa, in Europe, and throughout the Orient. Now it is becoming common knowledge that Sanskrit is the source the most widely-spoken languages of the earth.

Shrila Prabhupada writes about King Yayati, the son of Maharaja Nahusha, in his Bhaktivedanta Purport to *Shrimad-Bhagavatam* (1.12.24). Yayati Maharaja was, "the great emperor of the world and the original forefather of all great nations of the world who belong to the Aryan and Indo-European stock." Yayati had five sons, two from Devayani and three from Sharmishtha, namely (1) Yadu, (2) Turvasu, (3) Druhyu, (4) Anu and (5) Puru. From these sons of Yayati arose five famous dynasties. Spreading all over the world, these dynasties carried with them their Vedic culture and Sanskrit language, and the worship of the Supreme Personality of Godhead Lord Krishna, or Vishnu. As Vedic civilization spread, so did adoration of the demigods among materialistic classes.

By now, practically all the Vedic temples that once thrived in Europe, Turkey and the Middle East have been converted into mosques or churches. Yet, by spreading Lord Chaitanya's great *yagna* of the Holy Names all over the world, Shrila Prabhupada has become the prophet of a new tide of worldwide Vedic culture, and the catalyst for an emerging era of higher consciousness. Today, as I write these words, we are standing at the doorway of the Golden Age of Kali Yuga. It is due to the *sankirtana yagna,* which Prabhupada as the Acharya of the Holy Names introduced to the world, that old Vedic deities are once again resurfacing and making themselves known.

In a letter to a disciple dated 23 May 1968, Guru Maharaja wrote: "We should always know that Vrindaban is not localized in a particular area, but that wherever Krishna is there, Vrindaban is automatically there. And wherever the Holy Name of Krishna is chanted, Krishna is present there because there is no difference between Krishna and His Holy Name."

As world tensions increase, and the nuclear clock ticks towards the doom of nuclear midnight, we devotees must understand in our hearts that *tirtha yatra* means being "wherever Krishna is worshiped." Any spot that Shrila Prabhupada placed his foot became a *tirtha bhumi*. Times change, and past realities that have been swept away with the winds of fate may not immediately present themselves again. While we look ahead to the coming Golden Age with optimism, we remain cautiously aware that the years of transition to that blessed era will not be easy ones. These are times of *yugant*, the end of an era, and that can amount to destruction, in much the same way that the Battle of Kurukshetra heralded entrance from Dwapara Yuga into Kali Yuga. Although Krishna is everywhere, He is especially present where devotees worship Him by the grace of the shelter given by His pure devotee and world savior Shrila Prabhupada. There can be no higher *tirtha* than the place of Vaishnava *sadhu sanga*.

I am very grateful to my dear Godsister Shrimati Mayapriya devi dasi of Bookwrights Press for publishing this third, expanded edition of *Motorcycle Yoga,* which aims more for my devotee readers. When the first edition of the book came out two decades back, the once-renowned British marque Royal Enfield had declined into merely a local Indian brand run by tractor company Eicher. Since then, the storied company has introduced new models that have become so popular, that its 650cc Interceptor is expected to become the world's biggest selling large-capacity twin-cylinder moto. The first and second editions of *Motorcycle Yoga* were aimed at sharing Krishna-*katha* in a lighter mood with motorcycle enthusiasts, and those editions have fulfilled that purpose. With this third edition, I offer my thanks to all devotee readers for joining me in some motorcycle *yoga*. Ride well, but stay safe on your journey, back to home back to Krishna.

Patita Pavana dasa Adhikary (Miles Davis)
Sat-tila Ekadashi (25 January 2025)

CHAPTER ONE

Riding Bombay: 1981

"The Journey of a Thousand Miles Begins with First Gear"

AFTER SPENDING SOME FIVE YEARS in India and covering maybe half a hundred thousand miles on the sub-continent's buses and trains, in 1981 I got my first chance to ride a motorcycle there. Avatar Singh, son of a Bombay shopkeeper and my friend, asked me if I would like to pilot his Royal Enfield along the water-packed sands of Bombay's Juhu Beach. Riding a bike for the first time in ten years, finding the balance that comes with motorcycling once more, made for a perfect day on the water's edge. Noting my delight, my bearded Sikh friend made me an offer that I could not turn down. Avatar suggested that we take an all-day ride throughout Bombay. He would borrow his friend's Enfield and I would ride his. This would be no small task, for there was hardly a commotion on Earth that could equal Bombay traffic. Yet the chance to wheel through Asia's premier kaleidoscope port city was something I could not pass up. "Don't worry, Pavanji," Avatar told me calming my trepidation, "I will take the lead and you will stay out of trouble if you just tag along."

It is said in India that the taste of water changes every twenty miles and the "taste" in the dialect changes every forty. The rail traveler who boards a train in the Punjab and gets down the next day in Madras actually sleeps through several different sub-countries, old kingdoms, linguistic regions and a vastly changing geography. Riding that day with Avatar Singh, I discovered that a hundred miles by motorcycle was superior to a thousand miles by train.

Juhu, once a village where fishermen of mixed Portuguese and Hindu descent cast their nets, had by the 1970's grown into a prosperous suburb of beachfront hotels and Bollywood bungalows. Bombay too had once been a Portuguese colony, ceded by the Sultan of Gujarat in 1534. It fell into British hands as dowry in 1661 when King Charles II married Catherine of Braganza. History includes references to Bombay as Heptonesia ("seven islands") by Ptolomy, visits by Marco Polo (1298), and Vasco da Gama (1498), repeated raids by pirates like Captain Kidd in the early 1800's, and attempts by both the Dutch and French to colonize it. By the time the British succumbed to the Quit India Movement in 1947, Bombay had become a hopelessly congested magnet for the futile dreams of millions of poor villagers.

We discussed various routes. Finally I agreed to just follow Avatar and split lanes with him south through the towns of Vile Parle, Santa Cruz and Bandra, and into downtown Bombay. There we would pass the giant statue of Shivaji, the 18th century King of the Mahrattas, then follow Marine Drive into the bowels of the teeming metropolis. On the way we would see the cathedral-like, British-built railway stations of Victoria Terminus and Church Gate while riding through a hundred pages of history. We started out early the next day, wheeling through and around every sort of traffic snarl for an hour and a half until we came to the heart of the city. There we slowed down like victorious invaders and circled the block outside Crawford Market, a great indoor bazaar that was designed by Rudyard Kipling's architect father.

Here, where urban chaos reached its zenith, turmoil was redefined. *Brahmans* dressed in spotlessly clean white robes were rushing past the innumerable vendors and roadside filth on their way to worship Mumba Devi, the goddess who lent her name to the city. In the narrow gullis Mussalman tailors, bookbinders and perfumed oil merchants, with mustaches shaved above long black beards, plied their trades. Maharashtrian deliverymen were carrying steel tins of home-cooked meals to South Indian *brahman* accountants, whose wives could never think of their husbands eating at some ordinary restaurant. Olive-skinned Parsis in simple Western dress, followers of Zarasthustra of Old Persia, were greeting each other with a nod and "Sahebji." Short and pudgy Gujarati gold merchants, balding heads neatly oiled, passed by in tightly packed rickshas seated next to their smug wives, dressed in saris immaculately starched. The ricksha pullers, poor men from up north in Uttar Pradesh and Bihar, were bearing the burden of crushing poverty underneath another man's luxury. Yet neither had chosen to argue with the hand dealt by Fate. If there is one thing that all Indians have in common, it is an understanding of the laws of *karma*. Neither did I lament for one, nor condemn the other. The Laws of Nature are inescapably stringent and harsh, yet just. In this great samsaric go-round, he who receives must repay that which he owes either in this life or the next.

The season of *hemant* or winter only served to make Bombay's tropical weather pleasant. Nepali Hindus with brown faces reflecting an Oriental mien, were selling hand-knit woolen sweaters on the sidewalk, hoping for the rare cold snap. Descendants of Chinese cobblers were hurrying to their chop suey *dhabas*. Dark-skinned villagers from Goa with Portuguese surnames like De-Mello or DeSouza were rubbernecking like any visitor who gets to see a big city for his first time.

Crazy-glued in the endless traffic jam like everyone else, Marwari ladies—wives of wealthy merchants and industrialists—sat in chauffeur-driven Ambassador sedans gossiping about forthcoming marital alliances. They had stepped out of their Malabar Hill mansions to shop for things none of them could possibly need. On sidewalks and upon carts all about us, vendors were offering for sale, at ridiculously low prices, items I never knew existed. Young monks in saffron, the color worn by renunciates, were trying to discuss the message of the *Gita* with complacent shopkeepers who tried to get rid of them with the smallest possible donation. Jaded hippie tourists from America and Europe, playing *yogi* for a few weeks on the Goa-Bombay-Banaras-Kathmandu trail, tried to fit in with a crowd that preferred they proceed on their way to Thailand.

Long-robed Arabs, taxi drivers back home in the Gulf States, stood about importantly posturing as sheiks, and enjoying the power that their oil-rich currency would bring against the rupee. Gaping Buddhist tourists from Japan were there, too, to see and experience all aspects of a country where the founder of their religion walked and taught two and a half millennia earlier. As a Westerner I was dumbfounded to see the surprise shown even by other Asians at Bombay's measured disorder. Approaching the waterfront docks we noticed the occasional Russian and Greek sailor darting in and out of shops making a few last minute barters before shipping back out to sea.

We turned a corner just in time to be greeted by a somber crowd chanting "*Ram nam satya hay!*"...which translates: "Truth and goodness are found in the name of Ram!" Like marching soldiers on a mission, the crowd hurried past our bikes, now respectfully stilled, carrying a dead body wrapped in a white sheet, decorated in marigolds, and tied to a bamboo stretcher. Suddenly I found myself reflecting upon my late Sindhi acquaintance Mr. Mulchand, who in the days before partition had been a policeman in Karachi. Although Mulchandji was past ninety, we had grown to be good friends. One night Mulchand sent a message asking to see me. I sent back word that I would visit with him on the following morning. This turned out to be Mr. Mulchand's last night on Earth.

The next day I kept my word and I was one of those whose shoulder bore his remains to the burning grounds chanting *"ram nama satya hay!"* Old Mulchand and I were good friends, and as it is said, "A true friend follows his friend all the way to his last rites."

As Avatar and I circled towards the downtown residential areas, we found ourselves in the midst of a marriage procession complete with a marching brass band. The bridegroom, looking like a prince seated upon a dancing white horse, was on his way to claim the gold-adorned hand of his new life partner and have his own wrists manacled in iron. A few minutes later near the Gateway of India monument, we encountered an on-location film shoot. Perhaps no other scenario in India could have equaled the absurdity of Bollywood's movie making. The beggars had all been marshaled to one side, out of the camera's eye. The painted heroine was standing upon some hand-chiseled stone steps of a building screw-dancing and lip-synching to some blaring, screeching future hit song. Then, when the film would be released with much fanfare and ballyhoo in a month or two, the audience will be wooed into believing for two hours that poor people like themselves have ceased to exist.

Absurd, yet compelling, as things appeared that December day, Bombay's bald-faced contradictions continued to beckon like the mesmerizing wheel of life and death itself. I saw in that brown sea of humanity:

...the goddess-like beauty of young virgins laughing socially together while stepping over the distorted ugliness of poverty.
...the vast wealth of the privileged and the ability of others to subsist on nothing.
...the intoxicatingly sweet fragrance of night-blooming jasmine bushes wafting over horrible piles of refuse.
...the wisdom of sages and the ignorance of the faceless masses.
...the emerging middle class's eagerness to ape the West and the Old Guard's contempt of it.
...the ability of some to do nothing and yet be served by many, while others were spending their entire lives in service.
...the golden-toned Konkan *brahmans* passing by black-skinned tribals without so much as a glance at one another.
...the poor old lady whose job it was to pamper a rich dog.
...the power of human endurance and dignity which must stand up to a tidal wave of insurmountable odds.
...the whispers of past empires whose footprints, though shallower now, are not entirely blown over by the sands of time.

It seemed as though elements of all the three worlds and fourteen levels of the Universe were reflected there on the streets and alleyways of Bombay. For all that can be seen over time in India can be seen in a day's motorcycle ride through Bombay. At once comical, tragic, awe-inspiring and ridiculous, this show of generation, growth and dissolution that played before our eyes was running before we had arrived and doubtless continued to play after we turned our wheels to leave. Yet the seemingly impenetrable curtain of India had lifted for a day in celebration of my first ride there. I had seen people at opposing ends of the spectrum passing one another separated only by inches and yet by a rift as broad as a canyon. People from different eras had shuffled in and out of scenes as though emerging from a time machine or contrasting worlds. In this city of extremes—in caste, in education, in status—which revolves like some self-propelled velocipede of life, even the seasoned wanderer would grow bleary-eyed.

Back in America my compatriots would have been frittering away their days like some chosen few sampling the garden of delights. That is the way of the *bhoga-bhumi,* or "land of enjoyment," where the fruits produced of past good deeds are squandered like customers at a bank heedlessly withdrawing their money, without making fresh deposits. If America is the *bhoga-bhumi,* then India is the *karma-bhumi,* where the concomitant reactions to activities seem to make a more immediate stamp. The pious Hindu would rather suffer the mishaps of his misdeeds and mistakes in the here and now than be burdened with his heavy load in the hereafter. And here in Bombay, like no place else, will the soul swirling in the current of *samsara* be carried aloft by the incoming waves, or be drowned in the outgoing riptide.

Just as theatergoers watching a film flickering upon the screen are helpless to alter the plot, so the theater of Bombay stimulated my philosophical reflection. From a distance, separated by an invisible barricade, my unshared thoughts were mine alone. The rupee coin I dropped into the cup of the leprous beggar, to get him out of my face at a red light, had only served to insure that he would remain a beggar for another day. No amount of money can refurbish old *karma,* whose reactions are waiting to sprout like seedlings in spring. I had seen an endless show like some observant wayfarer just passing through. My rulebook had been left Stateside, for none of those restrictions would have applied in this world anyway. Realizing that my every twist of the throttle was as precarious as riding on an oil slick, I surrendered to the guidance of the Director of the stage, the Soul of all souls who has always watched each of us from within and without. In His hands alone are found the power to control the external and internal energies that harmonize all multifarious Universal forces. He alone can protect us from the reactions to our past errors.

The secret to seeing the Supremely Personal Force at work in all this passing parade is described in the ultimate text of *yoga*, the *Bhagavad-gita* 5.18. Therein Krishna advises *panditah sama-darshanah:* "He who is wise views all things with equal vision." He who knows this secret of *sama-darshanah* has attained equanimity, for he sees that the different types of bodies produced through the intertwining modes of Nature, or external energy, are the culmination of the past deeds of the doer. These modes of Nature, or *gunas*, are threefold: goodness, passion and ignorance. They alone are responsible for every type of body born of a mother, from a worm to a king. Yet each gross physical body is animated by an individual spiritual particle, each of which is a part and parcel of the Supreme Spirit Whole. The ride, the vision, the introspection: all had combined to make an incredible day of motorbiking.

Avatar Singh had apparently enjoyed himself too, going round and round from one bazaar to another. We had both forgotten to eat all day. As the Sun silently folded himself back into the Arabian Sea, Avatar motioned towards the *chat* and *bhel puri* stands along Chowpatty Beach. We parked the Enfields beside the curb and I walked alone over to the water's edge. Leaning down in the direction of the setting Sun, I scooped up a handful of seawater to sprinkle over my head in a silent ritual of self-baptism. I had become a rider in India on that day, and felt reborn.

CHAPTER TWO

The Road to Bhera Ghat
"Rolling with the River"

SHIFTING THE ENFIELD INTO NEUTRAL I glide to the pump at Jaiswal's petrol station, the only commercial enterprise for miles along this stretch of road. All around there is only lush farmland, unchanged since man first put plow to beast. I have been riding this road to Bhera Ghat for pleasure and my own inner tranquility for twenty years now, at least whenever I could tear away from America for the bosom of Mother India. Nothing has changed, including the Enfield, except for me. My only fear along this road to eternity is that this could somehow be my last ride. Since this road to Bhera Ghat represents ultimate moto-nirvana, I must ask myself to which world could the motorcycle *yogi* be promoted next? There can be no better ride than this.

Here on this stretch of National Highway 12, the Bhopal Road, there is a tunnel of huge shade trees lining either side. Ancient Indian kings, followers of the Vedic culture and heritage had these trees planted along these roadways to protect their traveling subjects from the harsh Sun and the elements. The gesture was not entirely a case of royal benevolence. It was important for the far-sighted monarch to facilitate travel. Caravans of trade that used this road for millennia provided a tax base that paid for the government's largesse. Each subject was expected to offer twenty-five per cent of his income into the royal treasury.

The Vedic king would also employ revenue acquired through taxation for religious ceremonies called *yagnas*. Because of these *yagnas*, prayerful fire offerings to Vishnu, the "All-pervasive One" was pleased to provide rain in season for His supplicants. Through measured rainfall farmers prospered and thus the kingdom was fed. The economy therefore was based upon religious sacrifices that brought rainfall, all overseen by a Maharaja. In the Vedic age the king was highly respected as the nara-dev, or "human representative of God." Indeed long ago some kings were themselves accepted as veritable avatars.

This Vedic system worked beautifully until invaders from Western Asia, and later Europe, pulverized India with demeaning physical and intellectual attacks. After 1,000 years of exploitation, India has been reduced to its present state, a third world nuclear behemoth, which boasts one out of every five engineers worldwide, yet stricken with poverty unseen elsewhere. Today India is a highly advanced, yet backward, land whose present cannot find the link that joins its past with its future. Confusion has become the national pastime.

It is not uncommon among first-time visitors to jump to the conclusion that India's indigenous religion has failed her. The truth, however, is that which really has failed India and brought her to this state is not following her eternal heritage. To some degree India can thank the generosity of ten centuries of foreign meddlers intent upon dismantling the oldest culture on earth. Of course, it would be un-Hindu for Indians to mete out blame, for they will explain it as the laws of *karma* at work: something done here in India must have first invited this cultural downfall. There can be no reaction without a primary action; some root misdeeds that have planted karmic seeds, spreading exponentially like so many garden weeds choking out the flowers. Apparently, when one's own culture is neglected, the door opens to other, sometimes unwanted, cultures.

These thoughts aside, today as I linger at Jaiswal's petrol station along the road to Bhera Ghat, it is as if the bloody tidal waves of looting, plundering invaders never came to wash this old land in red. These glorious old shade trees still shelter the wide expanse of the Bhopal Road. In the morning before the Sun's rays turn savage, the farmers till the soil made rich after evening rains. Brahmans on bicycles hurry just a bit to meet their appointments with temple deities, while mothers bathe their children at the wells set far from the road. In rotating eternal cycles, life goes on as it always has.

"Oi sahib," the attendant, Mr. Tiwari, casually greets me, although we haven't seen each other for a few years. He acts like I am among his most regular customers, as though only a week and a tank full of gas separates us from our last pumpside get-together. Like many Indians of the countryside, he appears to have an unspoken grasp on the eternal.

Tiwari fills the tank lovingly as though each ounce is liquid gold. I feel welcomed just by the kind finesse he displays making sure that the last drop falls into the reservoir, and that no careless splash stains the Enfield's chrome tank. My mind drifts to the secret places on the river's shore that will be mine to see in just a few moments. Some wanderers actually do feel affection for this crazy India and I am one of them. I have fallen entirely under the mystic spell of Mother India, and her rivers like the nearby River Narmada, just as though these very waters run through my veins. Mere kilometers from Jaiswal's petrol station are *ashrams* upon the riverbank in which austere *yogis*, drawing from the divine potency of the river's liquid goddess benefactress, cure the sick without medicines. There are places where avatars have meditated within the caves of the white cliffs above her emerald flow, and beneath her waves gods have entered into unknown subterranean worlds. Even today barefoot pilgrims circumambulate her entire length, a 1600-mile parikram over very rough terrain and among rougher tribals.

I have been struck by the region's simple beauty, for nowhere else on Earth have I experienced such tranquility. Today looking back, I can remember riding this road from Jabalpur to Bhera Ghat dozens of times, yet each ride had brought me face to face with something new. But then, in this strange land, even the commonplace becomes astounding.

Suddenly my mind returns to the situation at hand, the petrol pump, for a stranger is approaching me curiously. He is a traveler from Bhopal, judging by the license plate on his Rajdoot motorcycle. He is obviously from an urban environment, since he does not posses the villagers' shy and distant friendliness. This aggressive young man wants to show off. He has probably ridden here because of some business with the nearby medical college, though he does not have the pensive features of an Indian medical student. He is apparently unaware that his ridiculous greasy Beatles haircut, sideburns, sunglasses and bell-bottom trousers that embody the Carnaby Street look; faded away a few years before he was born.

He queries clumsily, "Have you ever been to India?" I can't but help finding this a bit too tempting.

"Yes, in fact, I'm there now." I reply, dryly mirroring his deadpan expression.

He keeps his composure: "I mean before...have you been there before."

"Yes, certainly, many *yogis* have told me that I was born there in my past life."

Amusingly, he shows no change in his composure except to take two steps backwards, while slowly wiggling his head. I wiggle mine to the same rhythm in reply as he responds by spitting out a huge red gob of *paan* all over the ground. Oh well, I joke with myself, enlightenment does not come easily. Besides I have managed to side step the two most asked questions. These are: "From which place you are coming?" and "Do you eat Indian food?" He refuses to even glance in my direction as he putt-putts off on his little two-stroke Rajdoot, which sounds like a well-played tabla drum. I'm not entirely happy about pissing him off. There are others here who actually do have a sense of humor. I tell myself, he'll get over it.

It is still mid-morning and a glorious day lies before me down the road. Tiwari locks my gas cap, takes the three hundred rupees and waves me a friendly farewell. I nose the Enfield onto the road towards my first stop, the temple of Tripurasundari Devi, literally "beautiful goddess of the three cities." These cities represent the three strata of this Universe: swarga or the heavenly world where the pious enjoy their rewards; naraka or hell where sinners get theirs; and the middle one of mankind called Bhumi-loka or Earth, where futures are decided quickly. She is also the goddess of the three modes—or gunas—of material nature, goodness, passion and ignorance. The goddess also oversees the three types of woes that arise from violating Nature's laws; miseries caused by others, by the body itself and by the *devas*, or demigods, who control Nature. Here within our limited citadel of the material Universe, it is she who reigns supreme as the "goddess of threes."

This area of the Narmada is famous for its *swayambhu*, or self-manifested, deities. The holy *murti* form of the Mother Goddess Shri Tripurasundari is said to have mystically appeared some thousands of years ago to one King Karna. She is unique in all of India insofar as she has three faces not carved by any hand. Her form reveals three of the goddess' many aspects: one face is Lakshmi, the goddess of wealth; the second is Saraswati, the goddess of learning; and the third is Kali, the "black" destroyer of the wicked demon Raktabija. I spot the jungle cow path to her temple off to the left.

As the Enfield finds direction, I am surprised to discover that the narrow jungle path to the temple has been recently paved. Later I am told that the state's chief minister, having heard of the once-obscure goddess and her glories, paid her a visit. As an offering to her, he had the rocky pathway turned into a solid strip of asphalt. Doubtless, the offering was made with taxpayer revenue and carried with it a prayer to the goddess that the minister be re-elected forever.

As the bike leads me along the new temple lane, a pair of humble beggars seated along the roadside catches my eye. A husband, in his middle years, sits peacefully upon an empty burlap bag beside his faithful wife. He bears the scars of some horrendous attack—someone has thrown acid onto his face leaving him blind and featureless. I discover some time later that the incident occurred over a Rs.250

debt. What is remarkable is how well cared for he is. His wife, an ever-loyal Hindu *dharma-patni* has kept him clean and well groomed. Though a beggar, she is in so many ways the typical Indian wife, known for her legendary fidelity.

If in India a man is found who is as focused upon God as half a billion Hindu women are devoted to their husbands, he is revered as a *mahatma* and is seated upon a throne. The Hindu patni is not content to serve her *patideva* only in this life, she wishes to join him in the next one, too. The well-known examples of Sati, Anasuya, Savitri and Damayanti, found in the historical epics *Mahabharata* and *Ramayana*, are dear to every Hindu heart. India's scriptures glorify those wives whose devotion has elevated each one to the venerable level of demi-goddess.

Similarly, in Rajasthan there is a temple built to a princess whose husband was killed by a band of brigands. The lady emerged from her covered palanquin to find her lord's lifeblood ebbing, sword still in hand. Prying the long steel blade from his still fingers, she fearlessly attacked the rogues, killing each one. She then collected a large pile of wood and carried upon it the body of her husband. Sitting with his head upon her lap, she lit a pyre and died as the flames rose, all the while stroking his forehead, and following her *patideva* to the next birth. Naturally, Westerners look askance at such extreme examples of single-minded love. Yet in this age of social liberation and the pretense of equality, the steadfast morality and unshakable devotion of the Indian woman hardly seems dented.

Some years back, while I was riding around Vrindavan and Vraja Mandala –a large area of Western Uttar Pradesh sacred to the *lila* of Lord Krishna–I chanced upon an unusual sight. There beside the River Yamuna was a frantic group of villagers hurriedly building a shrine. Stopping to inquire through an interpreter, I found that a young husband had died suddenly. His bride had immediately expressed her desire to perform the *sati* rite, or self-immolation upon the pyre of the husband, so named for the wife of Shiva who departed in a self-produced *yogic* fire. The *sati* rite has been outlawed for hundreds of years, ever since widows who had no desire to leave this world were forced to burn at their husband's funerals. Alarmed, the authorities informed the lady of Vraja that she would not be allowed to attend the funeral of her husband, and the police quickly confiscated his body.

Villagers building the temple narrated the following events to me. The authorities then tried to cremate his remains in a hidden area, but a sudden storm gathered and rain put out the fire. The police, exasperated, tossed the body into the river. As fate would have it, the body washed ashore some miles down stream, not far from the bereaved lady. Hearing that her husband's body was discovered nearby, the weeping widow rushed there and placed his lifeless head upon her lap. After several hours of meditation, self-combustion sprang from under her fingernails and toenails, and in minutes the two were consumed. I was given a photograph of the young lady for whom the shrine was now so fervently being built.

Pulling up alongside the beggar couple, I respectfully offer a Rs100 note. It's strange, but this is almost half of the debt that has now led to the couple's insurmountable suffering. The two of them are floored by a small offering of a little over two dollars. But then India is a land where peasants sometimes sell themselves into bonded labor to the village lender over a small loan. Many spend entire lives just working to pay off the interest. Before me, the thin asphalt line with its crests, curves and jungle serenity is the road-*yogis* dream. It ends quietly at the parking lot of the Temple of the Mother Goddess. First I park the Enfield, then I park my shoes, and walk towards the shrine.

The Three faces of Tripurasundari Devi, the goddess on the road to Bhera Ghat

Just then the temple priest passes by herding the cows which belong to the deity. The milk produced by these cows is used in the worship of Tripurasundari Devi. Milk is transformed into ghee for the fire offerings, into sweets like barfi and rasmalai, or into yogurt or cheese and placed before the Mother Goddess upon a silver plate. These cows will never enter a slaughterhouse; each one will be cared for in the temple *goshala* until her natural departure. The priest, Pandit Deviprasad, gently escorts the cows to their barn. Ten minutes later he returns dressed in his ceremonial *dhoti* with his fresh forehead mark of kum kum, signifying his devotion at the feet of the goddess he serves.

Since I have come from a great distance, and the pandit and I have known each other many years, he offers me a seat of honor in front of Goddess Tripurasundari. He blesses me by smearing kum kum powder with his right thumb upon my forehead, and drops three small spoonfuls of *charanamrita* into my waiting right palm. Literally "deathless at the feet of God." *charanamrita* is water that has washed the deity during the morning bathing ritual. It is mixed with sacred leaves from the tulasi plant and given as a sacrament to pilgrims as an elixir against the reactions to their bad *karma*. I drink it from the lower palm, from the *pitri-tirtha*, slightly to the left of where the fate line meets the lifeline. Panditji blesses me, *sarva papa vinasanam*. "All sinful reactions are now destroyed."

As Panditji prepares for the noon *aratik*, I get a peaceful moment's meditation upon the *mahamantra*. Within a few minutes, the bells and gongs awaken me from my thoughts. Devi Prasad has begun his offering of a ghee lamp before the Divine Mother Goddess. Joining the other pilgrims in unison we immediately spring to our feet, for not to do so would be disrespectful. As the ceremony progresses, it occurs to me that this site will one day become one of the principal centers of the Universal Mother, just like Vaishno Devi at Jammu, Sharada Devi at Maihar or Savitri Devi at Pushkar. Soon the sound of the blown conch shell signals the end of the ceremony, and Devi Prasad gently escorts me to the bike. Riding out on a cloud of bliss, I pass the beggar couple. The lady smiles shyly and speaks into the ear of her blind husband, who likewise beams in my direction through layers of dark brown scar tissue. I lean the bike left onto the Bhera Ghat Road. Perhaps the road to happiness really can be paved with bricks laid by acts of piety.

There is an analogy that likens those who worship the demigods and goddesses for material benefits unto prisoners who meet the lieutenant governor only to ask for transfer to a better cell. An intelligent prisoner should request the lieutenant to talk to the Governor on his behalf, and arrange for a pardon. He who prays for material benefits must also accept a material body with which to enjoy these "boons." The goal of *yoga*, of all worship, is freedom from this body and this world. Rebirth in the domain of the devi is the goal of the materialist, while the *yogi* achieves the Yogeshwar. I am riding headlong into the breeze now, a gentle wind that carries the fragrance of moist earth. Yogeshwar Krishna says in the *Gita*, "Among purifiers, I am the wind."

Mahankala Babaji of Parashurama Kund: Yogis are found off the beaten path in jungle hermitages, at river ashrams, and in their huts beside hidden lakes.

Soon a large *darwaza*, a cement portal, welcomes me on the left. Darwaza is an Urdu word meaning "gateway" that has found itself into the Hindi language. For that matter, it has also found itself into English in the word "door," though likely both find their origin in dwar from the world's oldest language, Sanskrit. I successfully negotiate the left turn through the Bhera Ghat Darwaza despite the accumulated layers of rocks, mud, sand and rubbish that make India's "highways" such a challenge for the motorcyclist, and pass through the gateway towards Bhera Ghat.

For the purpose of helping the pilgrim to reflect upon his spiritual journey, this door to the *dham* was constructed by a local committee. The pilgrim who passes through the door to a holy spot should mentally prepare himself. Prayerful acknowledgment of the Supreme Spirit who resides within and without all creatures in all species of life is the wayfarer's first duty. The concept of passing through one door as we leave this world, only to enter through another, is a concept found in all religious beliefs. The question that the Bhera Ghat Darwaza forces the pilgrim to reflect upon is, "Which door will I pass through next?" Internal prayer and reflection might inspire the answer, which could come from within.

Drawing closer to the Narmada the landscape appears to transform and I begin to perceive that I have indeed passed through the gateway to a mystical realm. Many of India's other sacred *tirtha-bhumis* have become exploited by charlatans, turned into carnivals complete with clowns in the dress of *brahmans*. Yet here motorcycling down this road it is different: this is Vedic society as it has always been, Earth's most ancient civilization tirelessly revolving in endless cycles. That which was the past is now the present and will become the future. Just as a tire going round and round occasionally throws out a pebble, sometimes the wheel of *samsara* releases the pilgrim seeker from the ever-circling *mandala* of continued birth.

The Narmada is a virgin goddess, unmolested and untouched by swindlers who make a living with their eyes upon the wallets of innocent pilgrims. She comes into view at her confluence with the Ban Ganga River. Genuine *brahmans* who reside by the river say that the mere sight of her flow is enough to obliterate the reactions to millions of past sins, what to speak of sinless pilgrims who come here to perform acts of devotion upon her banks. She is one of this magic land's seven rivers whose waters can grant release. A bath at Bhera Ghat prepares the pilgrim soul for the anti-material realms of eternal energy, the Vaikunthas, effulgent final liberation at last.

Bhera Ghat, in the Jabalpur District of Madhya Pradesh state, is approximately half way between the eight hundred mile river's origin and the place where she merges with her lord, the ocean god Sagar. Once Lord Shiva was passing through the hills that are now known as Amarkantak at the Narmada's source. Sitting down to meditate, he entered into a blissful trance. As a symptom of his ecstasy, Shiva began to perspire profusely. His sweat took the form of a daughter, a lady of great beauty and supple limbs. She was named *narma-dayini*, or Narmada, "the giver of happiness." The gods lusted after her and descended upon the earth to share her company. Desiring to remain a virgin, she outran the gods all the way to the sea, leaving the immortals (*amaras*) pulling thorns (*kantaks*) from their feet. Hence, the place of the Narmada's origin is called Amarkantak. There are said to be ten times ten million holy places at Amarkantak, where Narmada Devi is worshipped as a goddess who rides a crocodile.

In fact, there have been a few sightings of crocodiles reported locally. A boatman told me a story involving his friend and fellow boatman who was rowing a group of about a dozen pilgrims upstream to the Dhuadhar Falls. One of the passengers was carrying her child in her arms. To amuse himself the boy lowered his hand to splash in the river. Suddenly the toddler screamed, a crocodile had locked onto his little hand. The panicked mother called to the boatman for help, for no one aboard knew the river as he. The boatman grabbed the child from the arms of his mother, and threw him overboard. Later he explained that trying to wrestle the child out of the jaws of the crocodile would have been useless. The crocodile would have overturned the entire boat, and every passenger aboard would have drowned or have been eaten by other crocodiles.

The river is hundreds of feet deep here, and the ferocious reptiles are said to dwell on the bottom. Each time I have entered the river upstream it has occurred to me that it might be my last. But leaving this world as food for the mount of the river goddess would be superior to so many other forms of the inevitable exit. Yet I have never seen a crocodile here during my dozens of visits, though river snakes are quite common.

Riding alongside the Narmada, I soon enter the tiny village of Bhera Ghat and park the bike in front of my friend Mr. Jain's tiny shop. Mr. Jain vends marble sculptures to tourists who visit from all over India. He'll watch the Enfield for me as I have decided to hire a boat for a solitary ride up the river. As I turn towards the steps leading down to the river, a voice calls out, "Sir. From where you are coming, Sir." I turn to find a youth still in his teens eager for conversation.

I answer in clear tones affecting an Indian accent, to assure being understood, "From America. Now may I ask you a question?"

"Yes, Sir."

"Do you like Indian food?" I have the drop on him now, and the irony of my query–that he would never have tasted anything that is not Indian–escapes him.

"It is good, Sir. Too good."

"Much too good," I add. "It should not be so good.

"Why, Sir? How it can be too good?" I have his interest, yet his tone has changed to one of skepticism. He has told me himself that it is too good and now wishes to find out why it should not be so.

"Because of your tasty spices you had to endure Britain's East India Company for two hundred and fifty years."

"Quite right, Sir. It should not be that good." My new friend has a sense of humor.

A long flight of steps, perhaps a quarter mile in length, leads down to the riverside boat launch. Along the way, tiny shops sell marble sculptures of Lord Shiva, Hanuman, Lord Rama and other worshipful Deities of "Old Hindoostan." Most of the sellers are very poor, earning only a few pennies daily. I always eyeball each shop for *swayambhu lingas*, the self-manifested, egg-shaped forms of Shiva that the Narmada is famous for producing.

Once at the shore I no longer feel awe and reverence for the river, but rather the familiarity of seeing an old friend, one who keeps bringing me back. The Narmada is a friend all the way to the last, for who else would accept the burnt ashes of the departed looking to her for emancipation from *samsara?* Yet this is a friend whose steadiness one cannot rely upon entirely. Hence, the Sanskrit classics warn us, too much familiarity with rivers, as well as with women, kings or fire is unwise. Fortunately I have arrived in mid-June with the turmoil of monsoon season less than two weeks away. When the incessant rains come, and the excess water at the Bhargi Dam upstream will be released, this placid emerald stream will be transformed into a swirling, brown spate that only a fool would go near. The falls above Bhera Ghat will then disappear into an angry foaming whirlpool hundreds of feet deep. This pleasant jungle scene before me will be entirely transformed with the scheduled whim of Mother Nature, as we mere humans look on awestruck, yet powerless. Seeing the placid forest and peaceful river life, I make a note to return in a few weeks. Two-wheeling through a hot summer monsoon rainstorm is another experience of motorcycle *yoga* that has drawn me here.

A gentle boatman, whose entire life has been spent at this spot on this river, greets me warmly. For twenty rupees Krishnalal agrees to take me upstream between the towering marble cliffs, to the falls. Minutes out, as the river narrows, the world is mystically transformed, like entering into a quiet cavern. In cliff caves far above us, *yogis* through meditation sanctified this spot aeons ago. At Monkeys' Leap, Hanuman played with his friends at a time before Lord Rama requested these *vanaras*, or monkeys, to help Him defeat the wicked demon King Ravana. Shanidev, the lord of the planet of *karma* Saturn, came here to penance. So did the combined incarnation of Lords Brahma, Vishnu and Shiva, the sage Dattatreya, who long ago appeared as the son of Atri Maharshi and Anusuya. Indradeva, the thousand-eyed King of Heaven, dove into these waves with his elephant mount Airavata on his way to the nether regions far beneath the Earth. Villagers point to the shoreline mark of Airavata's huge hoof in the marble as proof.

As we wend our way upstream, I ask the boatman to pause at an island upon which *yogis* are still seen in meditation at times. On this small rock a 19th century queen, Rani Ahalyabai, installed a self-manifested Shiva-*linga*. Exploring the tiny rock island takes less than a minute. I bow my head to Shiva with the prayer *vaishnavanam yatha shambhu* and return to the boat. "Greatest of all gods and devotees of Lord Vishnu is Shiva!" Of the so-called "Trimurti." the three who control the Universe, Lord Brahma creates and Lord Shiva destroys. Yet only Lord Vishnu can maintain.

Over the ages, and from all over India, kings and wealthy merchants desiring to build a temple of Shiva have made the trip to Bhera Ghat, returning home with a self-manifested Deity, the Shiva-*linga*. The Shiva-*linga* is an egg-shaped black stone, sometimes bearing prehistoric, fossilized markings, found along the Narmada. How the Shiva-*linga* appeared at Bhera Ghat is explained locally, and also in the ancient Sanskrit literature, the *Puranas*. Once there was a great demon king named Banasura. He propitiated Lord Shiva upon the shore at Bhera Ghat by fashioning egg-shaped Shiva-*lingas* out of sand with his 1,000 arms. Finally Lord Shiva became pleased with Bana's austerities, and appeared to the demon king. "What would you like, my son?" the great god asked. "Oh Shiva, Oh Mahadeva," Bana replied, "Please turn all these sandy *lingas* I have made with my 1,000 hands into stone so that your image can be worshipped all over the world." Shiva smiled and replied, "*Tatatsu*. So be it." Riding upon his bull carrier Nandi, Lord Shiva departed leaving Bana with all his wishes fulfilled. Since then, this place has been called Banasura Ghat, shortened over time to Bhera Ghat.

Whenever I come here, I find several Shiva-*lingas* which, in fulfillment of Banasura's wish, I place in homes locally or abroad. Once I installed a small one about two inches tall in the home of a Maharashtrian widow. That done, I turned to her and said, "Your Shivaji is named Trimbakeshwar." so-named for a major temple in her home state of Maharashtra. The lady swooned and fainted, only her friend's catching her saved her from hitting the ground. As she returned to consciousness she confided, "My departed husband was named Trimbakeshwar."

Often, I am also proud of the fact that I have found or purchased three quite large Shiva-lingas, one of them weighing as much as fifty or sixty pounds, and have made local shrines for these around Jabalpur. Each one is in a public place, worshipped regularly, and can be visited today by anyone who cares to take the time. These small temples are Rameshwar in Adhartal, Pavaneshwar in Ashok Nagar, and Janeshwar at Damoh-naka.

To my sheer delight, from within Krishnalal's boat, the beauty of a Never-never Land comes to a zenith at the roaring falls. Krishnalal and I are the only ones floating here at the moment, so it is like having my own private showing of this mini-Niagara. This wonder of the world is one of India's best kept secrets, only a handful of non-Indians come here each year. Indeed, not that many Indians are aware of it, and of those who do come, very few know of its significance in the world of Puranic history. Rowing among the cliffs and into the chamber of the falls is an ascent into a mystical realm, whereas the return journey becomes a descent back into the routine of *samsara*.

At the boat launch, I pay Krishnalal, bidding him farewell as I ascend the stairs that lead up to tiny Bhera Ghat village. Every shop in the entire town specializes in only one item, marble carvings. The locally produced sculptures are mostly carved out of the soft marble, actually soapstone, from the cliffs that rise out of the river. Larger permanent deities are made from the much harder marble that has been trucked in from Makrana in Rajasthan, the same place from where the Taj Mahal's marble originated. The stunning detail and beauty of the deities of Hanuman, Sita-Rama, Radha-Krishna, Durga, Kali, Dattatreya, or of the river goddess Narmada seated upon her crocodile mount, makes me wonder how these spectacular artistic masterpieces were fashioned by simple village people, most of whom are assumed to be illiterates. Larger deities take several artisans working tirelessly all day for many months or longer to complete. The finished products are incarnations in stone whose beautiful faces reflect the loving hearts of the artists, men and women whose single-minded devotion to putting God's face on expressionless marble is obvious.

Turkish and Persian invaders considered such artwork as blasphemy, much like Afghanistan's now-defunct Taliban, which destroyed the beautiful 150 foot tall Buddha carved into the cliffs of the Bamiyan Valley. There is a temple above Bhera Ghat, over one thousand years old, called Sixty-four *Yogini*s dedicated to the many forms of the Universal goddess. Although the temple is still there and can be visited since it has now been granted historical protection status, it saddens me to go there. Each deity has been cracked, broken and desecrated by iconoclastic Persian and Afghan invaders. All *puja* has been halted at the temple, for the *brahmans* will not worship a broken deity.

The British, however, took a different approach in their zeal at dismantling Hinduism. The East India Company's method was to simply wear the Hindus down with arguments about their supposed backwardness and the impracticality of their religion. Certainly, in the British mind, the Indian was in every way inferior, but by becoming Anglicized, his poor lot could be improved at least a little. Under this charade, the British looted India, and then told the Indians that it was due to their religion that they had become bankrupt. British archaeologists would wax eloquently about old stone, marble or brass *murtis* if they were several hundred years old. Such purloined old *murtis* are found in indological displays in museums of London and the world. Like the Koh-I-Noor diamond, they were taken by India's "benefactors." Yet these same deities handmade today by the same technique is discounted as ignorant idolatry.

A British so-called "indologist" can authoritatively discuss an ancient Ganesh destined for some museum exhibit, yet the same scholar will transform himself into a modern, disapproving moralist when seeing the same Ganesh today take shape before the creative hands of *shilpis* for temple installation. Somehow the revelation of coming face to face with the oldest continuous living, breathing culture on Earth eludes the erudite scholar whose head is stuck in times that are lost. For him the past belongs to his sciences like anthropology and archaeology, but the present belongs to religious narrow-mindedness. Yet

I foresee that in 2500 years the same deities will be carved and ceremoniously worshipped while every theory of modern science will have been revised a hundred times like clockwork, and all paid for with government funds.

Under India's British educational system, modernization came to mean—and still means—rejection of thousands of years of rich heritage. *Brahmans* who once sang beautiful *mantras* in praise of the Supreme Absolute Truth were transformed into clerks shuffling around endless piles of paperwork. Traditional Indian dress was outlawed at government offices. A teacher of English received a salary twenty-five times greater than a Sanskrit *pandit* did. Still the British Raj brought undeniable advantages: building the world's most extensive railway, the English language or—closer to home—the Enfield motorcycle I ride.

Today the deities of Bhera Ghat that I am admiring are destined for temples all over India and abroad. I hope that wherever each one is placed for worship through the *pran-pratistha* or "life breath ceremony," their supplicants will no longer have to bear the hardship caused by prejudice and intolerance. Each one deserves to prosper and to give prosperity for a thousand years and more. And the Hindus themselves deserve credit for keeping their culture alive in the face of one thousand years of horrendous foreign onslaught.

Leaving the shops of the *shilpis,* I cross the packed dirt road to the waiting bike. I thank Mr. Jain for keeping an eye upon the Enfield, and kick-start its single cylinder for a ride through the town. At 15 kph Bhera Ghat village can be toured in its entirety in about five minutes. For the rest of the day I ride on throughout the district visiting holy lakes, cave and hillside temples. At the site of the fortress of Rani Durgavati, who was speared upon her elephant by Muslim invaders from Delhi, I reflect upon this young queen who married a tribal king and died for her beloved Jabalpur.

As the brilliant lunar crescent comes into view over the Vindhya Hills at sunset, the melodious vibration of temple singing wafts across the lake called Dev Tal. As I slow down to listen, I am filled with the sound of *akhand-kirtan,* endless chanting of the holy names of the Lord. I recall being once told that since this temple was built half a century ago, the name of Rama has been chanted here day and night without break. I pass out through the Bhera Ghat *darwaza* with the prayer that I will be called back once again.

The ride home is meditative and reflective. It occurs to me that except for a few ridiculous conversations about Indian food, I have hardly spoken all day. It has been a journey of meditative bliss on two wheels, a good day and a great ride. So good, in fact, that if I am called from this world here and now, I would leave entirely fulfilled and satisfied.

CHAPTER THREE

Kipling's India
"A Bubble Burst in Time"

NO WRITER, NO EXPLORER, NO ADVENTURER has ever enticed people on one side of the world to discover a culture on the other side like England's most esteemed poet laureate Rudyard Kipling. And no other work of literature has excited the world's imagination like Rudyard's *Jungle Books*. Woodsy tales of Balou, Sher Khan and Kaa have woven themselves into the fabric of western culture—in the form of postcards, comic books, cartoons, and full-length Hollywood productions.

A half century ago at my bedside my mother read to me Kipling's masterpieces of India. How my childhood imagination would soar! I wanted to run and play with Mowgli, the mancub; Balou, the bear; or Bagheera, the black panther. Kipling, with the eye of a sage, the voice of a master and the heart of a child, has done more than simply achieve an exalted pedestal in the world of literature. He has taught four generations about a secret India hidden deep within the jungles.

Kipling began the *Jungle Book* with the words, "It was seven o'clock of a very warm evening in the Seeonee Hills when Father Wolf woke up from his day's rest, scratched himself, yawned and stretched out his paws..."

While perusing a map of Central India on a train in 1981, in the maze of railroad tracks, roads and villages, I spotted a small town to the south called Seoni. *Seoni!* Something jogged an ancient memory long dormant. Could today's Seoni be the Seeonee of the *Jungle Books*? I showed the map to my fellow passengers, each of whom knew of Seoni (which the British spelled "Seeonee"). I learned that Seeonee of Kipling's *Jungle Books* is today the prosperous little town of Seoni in the southern part of India's Madhya Pradesh state. The town had taken its name from an ancient local temple of Goddess Shivani, the wife of Lord Shiva to whom Bombay-born Kipling would also write poetry. Over the years through local dialect and English influence the name had gradually changed from Shivani to Seeonee to Seoni.

Later I found that a 750 square mile area of jungle near Seoni had been declared a natural preserve called Kanha. In the early seventies, concern over encroachment had led the Indian Government under Indira Gandhi to create "Operation Tiger" for the preservation of the diminishing jungle resources. Kipling's India was alive and well!

Some time after this incident I developed a desire to undertake a solitary tour on two wheels of Seoni and the Kanha Jungle Preserve. At the time I was in Jabalpur, two hundred miles north of Seoni. My lone cycle tour would circle over half a thousand miles of central India's rolling countryside. This area being the most inland from India's two coasts was therefore the last to be explored by European colonialists. Indeed, even now in the 21st Century this vast and diverse province still harbors jungles from which even Indians are kept out due to the wild and deadly nature of the primitive *adi-vasi*s, tribal jungle dwellers following their own laws.

The scenic roadways of middle India offer the adventurer a potpourri of cities, villages, jungles and rural pastures. The natural charm is as enticing as any in the world. Madhya Pradesh is a peaceful place. There are no wars, no insurgency, no looting gangs of brigands that can be found in some of the country's disturbed border areas, where self-interested neighbors have been agitating ethnic groups on the other side of the frontiers into thoughtless, violent quests for unguided regional autonomy. Far from conflict, this is India as it always has been; the gentle pace of life vibrating warmly since time immemorial. There are no strangers—everyone you meet along the way is an instant friend. No two-wheeling adventurer who breathes central India's soft rural air and who reciprocates the warm greetings of villagers can avoid the transformation into a more timeless and transcendental mode.

After Siddiqui, my mechanic, tuned up and cleaned the Enfield, I asked Panditji, the astrologer, for a beneficial time to begin the trip. I needed a *shubbha-muhurta*, an auspicious moment of good stars under which to depart and bless the bike journey. "It had better be soon," I told him. The three-month monsoon season of the rains would be beginning soon. Kanha would be closing its green doors at the start of July's monsoonal onslaught, leaving the jungle's wild life free to roam, safe from the prying eyes of man. Panditji hurriedly examined his *panchang* stellar atlas and replied, "You may leave tomorrow when the Moon conjoins the auspicious Rohini star in Taurus." Offering him a few rupees I hurried home to pack the Enfield's saddlebags for the trip.

A steady ride to Kanha Preserve via Seoni would take six to seven hours. This was no Paris to Dakar run; the slow timeless pace of India demands obliging participation of the rider. Riding in India is a mystic and pleasurably intoxicating slow drift into another world. Neither can this land be gulped down all at once. It is no exaggeration to say that the motorcycle offers the third world adventurer the best means to see a country whose colorful people, tropical climate, spectacular views, wildlife and gentle rhythm of life bombards the motorcyclist's senses all at once. Yet the lullaby of a country ride in India can mask the fact that there are no roads on Earth more dangerous. During a recent two hundred-mile trip, I counted five fatal accidents along the way. Roads here are like the trees of the sandalwood forest: beautiful and fragrant, yet full of cobras.

At seven the next morning, I turn south onto National Highway 7. Under the bright morning Sun rising from behind the Vindhya Hills, activity is seen everywhere. Dairymen on two-stroke 175cc Rajdoots are putt putting about delivering scoopfulls of milk from the aluminum urns mounted fore and aft their bikes. A few truckers in their loud and unsightly behemoths are carelessly and dangerously careening all over the road with scant regard for the defenseless two-wheelers down below. Laughing students packed into rickshaws and onto bicycles headed for school—each in his clean but faded uniform—are unmindful of the traffic and danger all about them.

I ride out past the Jabalpur High Court and the Jaya Stambha, or "victory pillar" in its courtyard, erected to commenorate India's independence from the British Raj in 1947. This pillar has been said by some to mark this vast country's dead-center point, though recent geographers have placed the spot fifty or sixty miles north of here. The High Court was built by the British to resemble a gothic cathedral. In its yard barristers, dressed in the black jackets and white shirts of the British system they are still taught to emulate, stand about penguin-like discussing the day's cases they will present before the bench. Others are just pulling up on their Bajaj scooters, India's version of the Vespa. Barristers do not ride Enfields, which are preferred by the military and the police: Bullets are perceived as too macho for lawyers. One Bajaj scooter has been fitted in the rear with a extra set of twelve-inch wheels, an invention for a disabled man, and an innovation that might be tried with success in the West.

Riding through Sadar Bazaar, I pass the dilapidated, abandoned bungalows of long-gone English officers. Legendary British regiments like the Bengal Lancers or Grenadiers once did their exercises nearby at the Jabalpur cantonement. On the edge of the city, I spot the old British cemetery where I have often wandered just to ponder the fate of an evaporated empire that sprang up suddenly only to burst like a fragile bubble in history.

I find myself magnetically drawn through the gates of the British Cemetery like one who was buried here in some past life. The *chandala*, an Indian Christian guard in charge of the yard, pleasantly greets me at the gate and tells me, "The rains have caused the grasses to grow tall hiding the older graves. The cows and goats will soon be brought to trim them. For now, there are cobras hiding there." His smile turns sly as he adds, "Should you enter here, Sahib, you may not be able to leave."

Why have I stopped here anyway? It was Kipling who coined the expression "white man's burden." And now all the colonialist hoopla of the mighty British Raj has come to this, a British cemetery, while India limps and struggles ahead into the 21st century. Kipling called Victoria, the absentee Queen-in-mourning, "the Widow at Windsor." an expression that "did not amuse Her Majesty." Kipling, too, wondered, "We don't know why we are here." Would Kipling himself be amused to see these crumbling gravestones of Englishmen who died without knowing what they were doing here?

A few years ago, while walking upon trimmed grass amongst these fossils of a lost empire, I sat down and penned the following poem:

White Man's Graveyard

Sergeant Major Matthew Moore
Drowned with his horse in the River Gaur.
He died quick and he died hard,
Here in the white man's graveyard.

Cholera came in the dead of night,
Sixteen soldier's souls took flight.
From British soil ever barred,
They lie in the white man's graveyard.

Malaria came in '89,
Before the discovery of quinine.
A road was paved from the nurse's ward
Here to the white man's graveyard.

Ghostly voices rise from graves
With one tongue they seem to say,
"Why we came, we'll never know
Empires come and Empires go.
We faced bullets, plague and sword,
To lie in the white man's graveyard.

The sun never set on our Empire
But to raise the Jack we've walked through fire.
We gambled all and drew death's card
To win the white man's graveyard."

Today the rays of the Sun rising gloriously on my left dance upon the headstones of ancient gravesites as I wend my wheels away from the past and head out towards the inescapable living beauty of central India's countryside. About four hours out, a little before noon, wisps of bluish-blackish clouds begin to gather together and hover over rich fields. The scent in the wind tells me that soon I will witness the handiwork of Indra, the god of weather. It looks as though this year the monsoon will start on time. I make a quick guess that it will be more expedient to try to outrun the gathering storm than to take shelter and risk getting caught in the middle of nowhere in case the rains last till nightfall.

As the three-month monsoon season progresses, rainfall will become more severe and storms more intense. Racing over a windy bluff I reflect back to a July bike trip a few years earlier. Out in the middle of nowhere, an angry storm suddenly churned up all around me. Giant black clouds had gathered with such profound force and ferocity, I felt they were singularly seeking me out. A storm as vast as an ocean seemed to sit on my shoulder as huge pellets of water shot through my bike and me from every direction at once. No shelter could be found anywhere, under neither tree nor bush. I was drenched and had to pour quarts of water from my boots every few minutes as the storm clouds stalled against hillsides. Soon I had to battle my way up to high ground to escape a flood's torrential flow.

On other occasions, a more gentle cloud would titillate and refresh me with the lightest spray of water. Within a few minutes the Sun would reappear in full glory and without even slowing down the bike, the mist would bathe me and even launder my clothes while the joyful Indian Sun would dry me. Today, by good fortune and a shift in the wind, this rainfall never reaches me as I watch the clouds dwindle in the distance.

By evening time I have passed through villages, towns, forested hills and fertile countryside; and have felt the timeless beat of central India's heart all along the way. As I arrive at the Kanha jungle outskirts via the town of Seoni, the sky is the color of a Ceylonese sapphire. The Sun as it sets in the West, is followed by a glorious sliver of a newly waxing Moon conjoined Saturn and Jupiter. I had booked reservations in a log hut two miles inside the park. Since no two or four wheeled private vehicles are allowed inside Kanha, tomorrow I will hire an elephant. At nightfall began the wicked chorus of laughter from a bloodthirsty gang of hyenas, so despised by the other animals, making me glad for the iron bars on the windows.

The next day I join a group of four or five others, all Indian tourists. Our elephants are Kamala, a female named for the lotus of Goddess Lakshmi, and Badal, a male whose name means "cloud." In Kanha the mahouts have a rule that no procession will venture into the jungle without a male lead elephant, for it is the male that the tigers fear. Further, the elephants are not allowed to follow those tigers that have not recently feasted, as evidenced by a nearby carcass of some unfortunate deer. Not long ago, quite by accident, the son of a mahout slipped from the wooden *palki* atop the elephant. Before he hit the ground, he found himself locked within the strong jaws of a tiger. Sometime later, the child's remains were found in the jungle.

Kanha's elephants and their *mahouts* know every tiger, every Sher Khan, within the jungle and daily stroll fearlessly amongst them. We will be safe too, no matter how close we get to the tigers, as long as we stay on top of the elephant in the *palki*. To walk or ride alone in these woods would be foolish. The four-hour ride atop the elephants brings me very close to many forms of wildlife: tigers, laughing hyenas, families of wild boar trotting in procession, a few black bears, snorting Indian buffaloes, languor monkeys in every tree and many unusual species of deer. Here and there we spot the huge jungle ants have built hill-like mud hives, some over four feet high.

Our elephants carry us into a deep dry gully where, upon the gully's bank, we observe a tiger at eye level. Not six feet away the tiger yawns, stretches in the Sun and rolls over playfully. Sher Khan shows me his fangs before abandoning the gully reluctantly. Kamala and Badal appear to smile, overjoyed at putting a tiger to slow chase. No doubt they have done this hundreds of times.

That night in the hut sleep is profound amidst the hypnotic jungle chorus. The next morning I decide to return to Jabalpur on another route traveling via the holy town of Mandla. Turning onto the Mandla Road, I spot a group of men staring at some object laying by the wayside. Curious, I pull over to see what has atttracted so much attention. Leaving the Enfield on its sidestand, I gently elbow my way to the front of the murmuring crowd. To my surprise this gathering of country gentlemen, farmers and laborers is standing at a respectable distance from ... an ordinary truck tire! As I lean over to see what has fascinated them about a rubber tire, a hand grabs my arm and pulls me back. From the tire's center rim the shiny head of a black cobra emerges–gingerly at first, but turning menacing very quickly. As the cobra expands its hood, the crowd takes a long step backward in unison. The *naag* quickly rotates 180 degrees catching sight of every eye in the crowd, leaving no one any thought about picking up the abandoned tire.

Down the road a truck slowly approaches, then stops. As the driver exits his vehicle to join the on-lookers, it is apparent from his excited Hindi that this is his tire. It has fallen off the rear of his flat bed truck just minutes earlier. He had swerved to avoid this very cobra which had been crawling across the road. To everyone's amazement, the cobra, upon spotting the truck and its driver, deflates his hood and silently slithers off into the woods, like a sentry whose shift at guard duty has just ended. A dignified grey-haired man in the crowd, perhaps a village teacher, turns to me and in chaste English says, "He will find his own way."

It is no wonder that living here in India, Kipling could write about the creatures of the jungle distinguishing each according to its own personality. Many will recall from the *Jungle Book* the wise old treacherous cobra named Kaa. It is said that Kipling coined the name from *kaala-naag*, Hindi for "black snake." Kipling wrote, "Kaa was everything that the monkeys feared in the Jungle, for none of them knew what limits of his power, none of them could look him in the face, and none had ever come away alive from his hug." Yet even Kaa must have a sense of justice.

Here in the magic India of Kipling, sometimes even the Sun, Moon and stars appear to be like living, breathing watchers over the natural world below whose participants interact socially in friendship and enmity as do you and I. From time to time Mother Nature may open her door and allow man a moment's participation. The crowd disperses silently, each man going his own way as the trucker retrieves his tire by Kaa's will and continues on his way. And I am stunned into a thoughtful silence as I return to kick-start the Enfield and find my own way home here in the India of Kipling.

Sher Khan growls and slowly disappears into the jungle of Kanha

CHAPTER FOUR

Around Damoh
"...Of Dogs and Men and Demi-Gods"

THE ENFIELD FISHTAILS AS I SLIDE to a stop on the pebbles at a heavily trafficked intersection. Rows of soot-encrusted trucks carrying crushed stones stand here like elephants passing their time, snorting at each other. The large granite chunks they carry from local quarries are used for building roads–yet there is hardly a road beneath their huge still tires. Constant heavy trucking and torrential monsoon rains have ground the thin hand-laid asphalt ribbon that once lay here into little more that dried mud. Nothing is permanent anyway; as the road once was, so it has again become.

Marking the dead center of the crossroads is an unfortunate stray dog, who some days ago had carelessly wandered amidst insensitive giant wheels. He has been rendered into a sort of mangy dog-skin rug and now only a flat stretched-out four legged pelt remains of him. The trucks are all Indian-built Tata diesels. For protection, many have the grinning face of a rakshasa demon painted on the differential housing. Others sport an old shoe dangling from the bumper. Yet, judging by the mishaps caused by these giants, I doubt the efficacy of these measures.

Hand lettered upon the rear gate of each one is a slogan that reads "Horn OK Please" or "Awazd" (make noise). What noise on earth could rise above this din? A road sign reads DEAD SLOW WORK IN PROGRESS. Without punctuation, I provide my own interpretation since these trucks can grind a road into pebbles before the asphalt dries. Rather than dead slow work, road building is an eternal process like the slow march of the soul towards moksha.

I rev the bike's engine menacingly at the Tatas, but it is only for my self-amusement. I could slog around them on the left by sloshing 19-inch Dunlops through a 12-inch deep bank of mud, but I'd rather not get my shoes and tires weighted with wet earth that's better left and needed where it is. Besides, I am merely a wanderer just passing through and I need no mud clots as souvenirs. My wish is to change nothing and meditations will be my mementos. In any case, if the bike weighing 370 pounds plus me on it sinks half-wheel deep in quick mud, it will be a near-impossible mess to extract.

Beyond the four-corners of this miserable crossroad lie green rice fields covered by a serene mirror of still water. In one of the fields a dozen or so women in gorgeously colored saris of red or green or blue are bent over planting the paddies, innocently displaying a row of round buttocks to the road. White cranes stand about socially off to the side; sharp eyes and ears focused at the shoots for frogs who surface to hear themselves croak. The frogs are not unlike me who sits here, respectfully wary of the Tatas and idly revving my Royal Enfield's single cylinder, wasting precious petrol just to hear the sound. Off to my right a mother rhesus monkey, her baby clinging tightly to her back, makes a mad dash up a tree. The baby rhesus gives me a fearful look as the two disappear into the branches. Instinctively, I remove my sunglasses, lest one of her associates drops down from behind and tries to steal them.

A flock of green parrots dancing through the sky on my left zig zags and merges with another group that flies in from my right, and they all wing off together one hundred strong, into the clouds. I spot a momentary gap that suddenly widens in the line of trucks ahead. Pushing the gear lever into first with my right foot, I twist the throttle and quickly release the clutch. At 18hp the 350cc Bullet doesn't exactly do wheelies. But what it lacks in immediate response, it makes up for in reliability. With some gritty effort and derring-do I snake through the man-made truck jungle praying not to end up under giant wheels, as has unlucky brother dog. Racing around towering trucks, I blast my horn in submissive obedience to their painted "Horn OK Please" admonitions ... as if any of the drivers could hear my noise above the wind, smoke and diesel engines of this brutal manmade hell, just mere meters from a natural green paradise.

Breaking free from the mob of megaliths I gun the bike through the three upper gears until the speedo shows 65 kmh upon a stretch of paved roadway. I must put some space between the bike and any of the trucks that are lumbering after me. When roads narrow to the width of one lane, the Tatas can be impossible to get around and precious life in this land of one billion quickly becomes cheap. Cheap, that is, in the estimation of others. Even an insect, like an ant or a fly, will try to save itself and I am no different. "Die Trying" may seem like an impressive sticker plastered on the bumper of some grotesquely overbuilt SUV back in California. No one wants to die unsung and alone in this third world. Indeed, death has but few volunteers.

It is not wise to cruise any faster than 65 kph though the Enfield is comfortable at speeds up to 85 kph. Roads can turn treacherous in a heartbeat, and out here the only ambulance could be a bullock cart. Finally confident that I have somehow outdistanced the Tatas, I slow the Bullet down to forty-five to absorb rural India's countryside ambience. As I summit the crest of a hill, a fertile valley lies before me. The soft gentle breeze turns a bit stiffer up here, perhaps hinting a promise of coming rain. It is the monsoon season now, though the last storm was two days ago. Here atop the bluff the terrain is rockier and the soil redder than in the lush valley. On either side of me are dense forests of large-leafed teak trees.

As the road gently undulates down through the fertile fields into the valley, I spy a lone farmer guiding an ancient wooden plow behind a huge white bull. The observant traveler through India's countryside learns early on why the cow and the bull are so revered here. By his steady and patient plodding the bull provides food grains, while the cow gives her milk in exchange for mere grass. Milk, the staple diet of India's largely vegetarian countryside folks, figures into an uncountable variety of recipes: *dahi, khir, paneer* and hundreds of milk sweets. Eighty-five per cent of India, Hindus as well as many others, will not eat beef. Indeed, it is difficult to explain to someone living in another time and clime, but here at least you find yourself in awe of the bull's nobility, plodding through eons of changeless, yet ever-changing, civilization. Maybe for me it is a bit more obvious since I have been a vegetarian since my teens. Now a national movement to ban cow slaughter is gaining power and I have no regrets that I, too, have marched with protesters chanting *go-hatya bandh karo* ("ban cow slaughter") here in India. The farmer returns my wave as I slowly pass by. It is certain that his bull will never see a slaughterhouse.

Anchored behind the span of chrome handlebars and surrounded by winds and living nature, rather than within a windowed cage submerged in an artificial climate, it becomes easy to appreciate this land. India's natural beauty could be reflected in many places of the world, like the rich agricultural valleys of Northern California or Southern France. Yet there is a big difference. Although the Sun has pushed the mercury to the mid-seventies and the morning sky is dazzling and bright, the monsoon air hangs rich and heavy with a soft tropical wetness. Suspended moisture of the season of the rains caresses the skin and even leaves the inner spirit refreshed. Here in the Madhya Pradesh countryside you feel the soft breath of eternity, life as it always has been in balance with Nature ... once, that is, the trucks have been left behind.

Perhaps the biggest difference between riding in the West and riding in India–*riding* India–is this overpowering and all-encompassing awakening which grasps the eternal. Here, it seems as if that which is beyond the world of death reaches down, encompassing the road-*yogi* with his every breath. This is the knowledge of transcendence that emanates from within every penitent *sadhu* that I bow my head to as I ride by. Immortal India is a land whose timeless history has never been appreciably described by modern scholars. They who are so limited by time will never appreciate timelessness. From an objective point of view, the only real and proper texts describing how India got to the here and now of today would be this land's own historical Sanskrit texts. Even today, the one-hundred-thousand-verse long *Mahabharata*, the *Bhagavad-gita* being a small part, is known as the world's longest poem. Yet it is so much more than mere poetry: it is literally "the great history of India, that was known in ancient days as Bharata."

Modern speculations regarding India's roots and culture are mere theories, many of which were designed by invaders. Profiteering colonialists with their divide-and-conquer agenda, as well as patronizing modern so-called historians, have disallowed the old and indigenous texts of Mother India from commenting upon herself or her origins. In fact, the Holy Scriptures of this land have all been neutered by one word, "mythology." Serious research and study of the Sanskrit texts has been condemned and ignored. Instead, with the sole intent being the social subjugation of India, the phantasmal, dishonest and–according to the Sanskrit histories–entirely unfounded "Aryan Invasion Theory" has been inserted into the history books. Undoubtedly, this ridiculous theory is one of the biggest concoctions ever to have been thrust upon an innocent population, yet hardly a whimper has been raised against it.

Entire histories of races, of dynasties, of religious schools of thought, and of the many sciences that accompanied the rise of the Eastern civilization have been stamped as fantastic and unbelievable mythologies. Many of these "authorities" having never visited India, let alone ridden through her countryside or having sat before her *sadhus*. Modern atheistic science cannot explain how many astounding and purely scientific principles, as those freely discussed in the *Puranas*, have arisen from the "superstitious minds of India's underdeveloped peoples." Early British indologists like Sir William Jones appreciated Sanskrit as the mother of all language, though later colonialists whited out this fact when they saw it did not suit the business of colonialism. Indeed, it is the Sanskrit influence that has given the world even basic ideas like the measurement of time, even though the link to India has hardly been appreciated. Even the Vedic concept of *kala*, or time, is the father of the modern calendar, the *kalandar.*

Remember those wise men from the East that blessed Baby Jesus? They were from India, where gold, frankincense and myrrh are still sometimes offered to new mothers. Amazingly, the birth and life of Jesus have been foretold in the *Bhavishya Purana,* long before the Jewish Prophet appeared to teach the West love of God. Bhavishya Purana goes on to tell how Jesus escaped the crucifixion, taking shelter of Kashmir. In Shrinagar to this day his burial site is pointed to as Rozabol, "tomb of the prophet," atop Shankaracharya Hill. Truth is stranger than fiction, Bubba, and India's history is the strangest truth of all.

That which lasts forever cannot be destroyed, and that which begins must meet its inevitable doom. Entire civilizations once expected to rule the Earth forever have crumbled and have been forgotten, as the sands of time sweep over the graves of former kings. Darwin's misguided theory has tried to show that we all descended from the monkey, whose relatives caused me to hide my glasses a few miles back. Yet there are no monkeys in upper North America, except in zoos, so how did man get there? Right, the entire continent broke away from somewhere else and found a new home, leaving all the monkeys behind. But then, why aren't those zoo-monkeys giving birth to baby humans?

We are taught an imperfect science that has drawn many conclusions over the past few decades that are now forever engraved in stone. One by one, old theories crumble, only to be replaced by new "everlasting," government-funded theories. Yet there are to this day places upon this very Earth that remain inaccessible, and about which we haven't a clue. We explain that it is the Earth's "gravity" that keeps these two wheels rolling upon the road, yet no scientist's test tube has produced an ounce of this invisible thing that they have named as gravity. Likewise, the sweet morning dew has been named "condensation," as though that answers that. But why has an atheistic science become too miserly to give credit to the Earth Mother? It is she who gently waters the plants, the greenery that cleans the air for us who pollute with inventions and ideas.

Every light must have a source, yet the awe-inspiring Northern Lights, science tells us, are merely "disturbed particles." For the faithful, these lights are emanations from the transcendental body of God, and they serve to remind us that there are questions that our empiricism cannot conceive. Thus devotion and faith–and not speculative atheistic science–are the keys to progress beyond the traps of body consciousness. Intelligence means liberating ourselves from ignorance. Useless scientific-sounding speculations are merely chain-like bonds to confusion. The seeker queries "Why is the sky blue," and the voice of the eternal answers "Because Vishnu is blue."

That which is spirit is deathless, and that which is matter must expire. Patanjali, the ancient father of *yoga* and the author of *The Yoga Sutras,* wrote in verse 2.5 "Nescience is misjudging that which is non-eternal, the impure, the painful, and the not-self to be the eternal, the pure, the pleasurable and the self." Everlasting pleasure is found in subordination to the Supreme Spiritual Whole. Sense gratification is not the goal of *yoga,* and neither should enjoyment of the body be considered as real pleasure.

The energies of the world, both those that are seen and those that are not seen, are basically of two types: internal and external. The external elements that comprise the bodies, in which we find ourselves daily growing older, are the changing, eight-fold material energies of *maya*. Though our actual identities are part and parcel of the internal energy or *yogamaya*, we are hopelessly embedded within the external forces due to having identified with the changeable. Only by our reverting to internal consciousness, finding within the original knowledge of He who is the Master of all energies, can the transfer to the domain of the spirit take place. The ultimate quest of *yoga* is realized in finding our eternal relationship with the Yogeshwar, Krishna, as told in the last verse of *Bhagavad-gita*.

The physical body, like the motorcycle, is nothing other than a mechanical device formed of the variegated elements of inferior energy. And like the body, the Enfield needs to take in fresh air through the carburetor and blow out exhaust through the pipe in order to function. The *yogic* principle of *pranayama* is no different. With each incoming breath the *yogi* draws in the life force of *prana*, then exhales when this force is spent. Just as the hands, feet and body control the motorcycle, so the spiritual spark, the *atma,* controls the body. That body in which there is no central spirit soul is like a motorcycle without a battery; it is a dead and useless object. *Yoga* is the means of awakening dormant spiritual consciousness. In fact, the strict definition of *yoga* is "to link." The *yoga* force links the practitioner with his higher self, then links the self with the Yogeshwar. When this linking relationship takes on the sublime mood of a subordinate, loving relationship with the Supreme One, then *yoga* has found its goal in *bhakti*. The mathematics of *yoga* is quite simple: one plus one equals One.

A little deep breathing–*pranayama*–to take in the landscapes of both matter and spirit, and I find myself transported into bike heaven. Excitement followed by bliss joins the ride like that which encircles the adept as he approaches the dawn of *samadhi*, and I feel suspended in time as though some other "me" is piloting the machine. I twist the throttle reflexively and, as my head slightly jerks backward, I awake transformed from eternal participant to foreign spectator once again. For a moment there I was submerged as one with this timeless land, and now I have rejoined my status as "wayfarer passing through." No longer suspended in transcendence, the wheeling *chakra* of *samsara* continues its spin and the trance of the fixed mind is lost. The road continues.

I am riding the blissful, yet terrible road to Damoh, a town I have wanted to visit for years, more out of idle curiosity than to sightsee. From a tourist's point of view, there is nothing in Damoh and the town is literally and figuratively beyond the middle of nowhere. But in this weather, this place, who could argue the destination? I am here for the ride, the motorcycle *yoga*.

Arriving in Damoh, I will most likely see that it reflects so many other towns of this vast belt of central India. The green countryside will probably end abruptly only to be replaced by a crowded, litter-strewn town that appears to be in a continuous state of unhurried crumbling. With a number of paint shops, there will hardly be one building that does not need painting. In the narrow lanes with no sidewalks, the pedestrians forced to walk in the streets will far outnumber the cars. With much work to be done in all directions, thousands of able young men may be loitering around dozens of tea and *paan* stalls. Wiring that looks like some electrician-gone-mad installed it, will perhaps be jumbled around electrical poles that stick out of the roadside at odd angles. There will definitely be men spitting red *paan* on the streets, while others urinate against walls painted with admonitions like, "DO NOT MAKE NUISANCE HERE."

India's traffic jams are not limited to motor vehicles!

How did I end up here on the road to Damoh? Over a dozen years ago beside the River Narmada, I obtained from a *brahman* at a place called Lameta Ghat, a large *swayambhu* Shiva-*linga* for the grand sum of twenty rupees. Somehow I developed an urge to install this deity of the Lord Destroyer under a *bael* tree at a crossroads in Jabalpur. Soon thereafter this Shiva stone was established beside a small temple of Hanuman under that very *bael* tree, with priests chanting auspicious Vedic invocations. This *murti-pratishta* took place under the second full Moon in spring, the night of Lord Buddha's birthday called Vaishakha-*purnima*. Behind this small city shrine, which stands to this day, is a working class colony. Daily the people of this colony perform the *puja* to Lord Janeshwar. They are simple religious men and women, the likes of whose toil carries this country upon their backs.

A few years after this *pratishta* I visited the shrine and found that out of gratitude someone had nailed a painted sheet metal sign onto the *bael* tree which translates from Hindi: "This Shiva-*baba* was placed here by an American *sahib*." Every time I pass by this shrine I am reminded of the gratitude shown by these strong-as-steel members of India's work force, people whose every breath appears to be drawn against all odds. I named the deity Shri Janeshwar, or "lord of mankind." Lord Janeshwar sits on National Highway 7 which runs from Benares, "the world's oldest city." to Kanya Kumari, the "virgin goddess" at the far southern tip where three great seas meet. This is India's "Mother Road" beginning at the home of Lord Shiva by the Ganges and running to Land's End where the Arabian Sea and the Bay of Bengal merge with the Indian Ocean. Jabalpur, the home of Lord Janeshwar, is at the exact halfway point, and marks the dead center of India.

There is a crossroads near Shri Janeshwar called Damoh-*naka*. This is the *naka* or "toll gate" where a fee is paid by truckers waiting to ply the Damoh Road. Thus for no particular reason other than breathing the air of the journey, I knew that someday I must make this trip to Damoh. Perhaps it is Shiva's will, but on a day when the *panchang* astrological calendar showed an auspicious date for travel, and my Enfield was in good tune, I left the teeming bazaars of Jabalpur behind. And that is how I now find myself embraced by the green countryside along the Damoh Rd.

Damoh is a little over 100 kilometers northwest of Jabalpur, a distance covered regularly by many commuters twice daily back in America. Yet here it is considered a long trip. A voyage of one hundred kilometers in this land of twelve hundred dialects can see a change in language, dress and customs. Due to the horrible conditions of the Damoh Road, a solid Indian Ambassador car must allow for a minimum of three and a half hours for this trip that, on an American highway, would be completed in air conditioned comfort in less than an hour. For the motorcycle *yogi* whose destination is always where he happens to be, this trip will take a few days or more than that. The morning is bright and cheerful. Puddles from the recent rain reflect the Sun's rays back to salute the sky.

I soon cross the mighty Hiranya ("golden") River via a submersible bridge. Only days earlier this flat non-barricaded bridge lay beneath four feet of water. Now the river level has fallen to ten feet below the bridge. The Hiranya, as many others I pass over on this day, has turned a muddy brown from the rains. Beneath the bridge in an eddy play a dozen or so chocolate brown village boys. On a dare from his friends one of them jumps from the river wearing only a sarcastic grin. He is nine or ten and, like the others, is completely naked. With his left hand he shakes "himself" in my direction as I try not to appear amused. The little daredevil cannonballs back into the swirling waters to the approval and laughter of his friends. Chances are, I am the first white man he has ever seen, hence the extraordinary greeting.

A few kilometers onward I cross a small and unnamed rivulet, the pristine appearance of which reflects one of the *Puranic* descriptions of *swarga* or heaven. The waters of this stream could be worthy of the sports of gods and goddesses in love. In my rolling quest after the elusive secrets of India the eternal, a sacred bath in her many waters has become an important ritual of *yoga*. Through the sub-continent run the seven major holy rivers, although many other streams are also considered sacred. They are practically all *nadis* or females, but a few are actually *nadas* or male rivers, like the Brahmaputra Nada in Assam. I have been the guest of India's waters for many decades now, so automatically the bathing *mantra* begins hypnotically revolving in my head. This is the song that turns all waters holy, water being essentially pure and, among the four gross elements, represents the *brahman* class. My mind sings:

gange cha jamune chaiva godavari saraswati
narmade sindhu kaveri jalesmin sannedin kuru

"The seven holy rivers that can confer liberation (unto he who bathes in their sacred waters) are: the Ganges, Yamuna, Godavari, Saraswati, Narmada, Sindhu and Kaveri."

By some great fortune, I have managed to bathe in each one of the seven holy rivers over time and can testify that each river goddess has her own personality and qualities. Emerging from a holy bath from a river, in the Bay of Bengal at Puri, or in the Arabian Sea at Dwaraka, or from the *sangams*–places where two rivers meet–the result is invariably the same. I am refreshed and renewed, and just a bit closer to understanding the heart of Mother India.

We are born from water and maintained by water as we live. For the Hindu, life ends not within earth but in waters that must accept his final ashes. From Gandhi to George Harrison, the Ganges has accepted the remains of billions, transporting the souls of the faithful to heaven.

Flat rock slabs flatly carved by the hand of God form a pathway through green grasses to the water's edge. Tapping the overhang of the rock with my foot assures me that no snakes, the spoilers of paradise, are lurking unseen. In spite of being alone, I feel no fear. Wearing only a loincloth, I have left my clothes on the shore. The water is warm, soft and inviting. The rivulet embraces me with its high energy as I dog paddle to the center where a submerged boulder becomes my holy *asana*. It is no wonder that in this land rivers are worshipped as personalities: loving, benign and caring. Like a mother, the river goddess embraces us; washing our bodies and making us fit for social contact, never being repulsed by our uncleanliness.

As I become accustomed to my submerged throne in the river, a school of hundreds of curious minnows surrounds me. I feel like a member of their social circle. My new friends are only two or three inches long and have large curious eyes. It is the noon hour now, and time for the *gayatri mantra* meditation. In 1969 when my Guru Maharaja offered me *diksha* or initiation, he draped a *brahman* thread from my left shoulder around me to my right torso. This is the *yagnopavit*, the six thread-loop worn by the initiated *brahman*. As per tradition, I wrap the thread around the thumb of my right hand. Silently I recite the holy *gayatri* prayer to the Sun god, counting *mantras* upon my fingers. *Om bhur bhuvah sva tat savitur…*

The Sun is the source of life for all the three worlds. The brilliance of the Sun in this our Universe, one Universe among many, represents only a small fraction of the overwhelming light of the Supreme Lord. To help the *yogi* understand the brilliant light of the Godhead, He who is supreme, the *Vedas* instruct that His effulgence equals millions of suns. Cognizant of the power of that all transcendent light, there are many spiritualists–Shaivites, Jains, Buddhists, Sufis and other. They set their goal upon obliterating all sense of egoism in order to merge with God's all-encompassing spiritual light, His *brahma-jyoti*. My Guru Maharaja instructed that it is even higher still to go beyond that light, to the personal form of the Supreme Lord Shri Krishna. To underscore that point, he taught this *mantra* from *Shri Ishopanishad*:

> *hiranmayena paatrena satyasyaa pihitam mukham*
> *tat tvam pushann apaavrinu saatya-dharmaaya drishtaye*

"Oh Supreme Absolute Truth, sustainer of the Universe, Your beautiful face is covered by Your golden effulgence. Please unveil the dazzling curtain of Your light and let me, who am purely devoted unto You, behold Your form of bliss."

My Guru Maharaja, Srila Prabhupada, did not deny that the all-transcendent Supreme Lord is the source of the *brahmajyoti* or the "white light." He urged his disciples to go beyond merely merging with that spiritual light to the lotus feet of the Person Godhead. Above the act of merging the self into an ocean of light is discovering our eternal and reciprocal relationship with the Supreme Lord based upon our willingness to serve Him. Eternally liberated souls or *moksha-jivans*, having achieved the goal of *yoga*, reside in a world free from the fear of death and rebirth in a spiritual, anti-material universe beyond this one. That supreme abode is called Vaikuntha, the "place where there is no fear." My Guru Maharaja did not advise the frustrating attempt at extinguishing the ego, as urged by many so-called *yogis*. It was my spiritual master's challenge that each of us discover within the eternal and spiritual real ego. This is the *atma*, the spiritual self which transcends this concocted, body-based material personality. Having founded our sense of who we are based on our physical shape, race, age, nationality, religion and other temporary products of material inebriation, our vision of the transcendental self within has grown dim. Our original and unique spiritual personality, from which the materialistic ego is a warped reflection, lingers asleep behind a wall of *maya*, illusion. Discovery of the Lord of the Heart, the Self of all selves within the very *atma* particle awaits those eyes that have turned inwards. And today motorcycle *yoga* also means my inward journey to the soul, and unto the Soul of all souls, the most courageous trip of all.

A journey to lost horizons

Since God's gift of this human form of life is temporary and must not be wasted, it behooves us to make progress in *yoga* while we can. Defeat alone can be expected if life is aimed at trying to enjoy a gross physical body that is doomed to perish from its very birth. My Guru Maharaja taught, "Develop spiritual assets by serving Krishna, for real wealth can never be taken from you. All material wealth and opulence ends with this body. *Daivi sampath* or eternal wealth will journey with you beyond this life and into the next. Your temporary fame, fortune and social standing will be finished when this life's journey is finished. Your body will become the food for jackals, worms or fire, this is certain. Map out your journey for the trip back to Godhead."

Completing my *gayatri mantra,* I offer due obeisance to God and *guru*. *Mantra* literally means *mana-trayate* or "that which delivers the mind." The fish nibbling upon my body, their good company notwithstanding, have not assisted me in savoring the full mind-elevating power of the *mantra*. I feel like the great ascetic Saubhari Muni, whose river meditation was spoiled when fish began to tickle his body, awakening his latent desire. As a result, he soon found himself married and entangled hopelessly in the world of in-laws and offspring. But was it my imagination, or were the fish attracted to the tattoo of Lord Krishna on my right arm?

Glistening in the Sun, the chrome fender of the Enfield catches my eye. The bike stands waiting loyal, royal and ready to boil. Now with my bath and *gayatri* meditation completed by the grace of the Sun god and the river goddess, I dress quickly and return to the saddle, rejoining the road to Damoh. With a quick glance over my shoulder I see that a herdsman from somewhere in the forest has arrived with more than a dozen big black water buffaloes that one by one lumber into the stream. By divine will I had left the water just in time.

India's simple village life

A few months back in April and May, before the onset of the monsoon rains, this land was scorched by temperatures that could sometimes exceed 115 degrees. Now fields made productive once again by the seasonal cycles stand bursting with grain, obscuring peasant huts of mud and straw. The hues of the soil are reflected in the bricks of the houses: as the color of the land changes from brown to shades of red over miles, so does the color of each hut. Passing through the tiny village of Patan, I continue onward. The bike is holding a steady 45 kph while my mind is holding onto the *mahamantra,* the true sustenance of the journey.

Soon I am overlooking a huge fertile valley divided by the gentle flow of a small stream. Off to my right, about three kilometers below, proudly stand the painted white spires of an old temple beside the river's edge. A pleasant slow ride into the valley brings me to a *darwaza,* or gateway. It reflects a recent design, one that is engraved with a Hindi greeting, a welcome to a Jain *mandir.* The Jains are considered by some to be a "branch of Hinduism." but the Jains consider themselves to be entirely separate. In truth their roots are found in the scriptures of Vedic India. As described in detail in the *Shrimad-Bhagavatam,* King Rishabhadeva was the first of the twenty-three Jain *tirthankars,* or holy teachers. He is called Adinath, the "first Lord," by the adherents of this austere sect. King Rishabhadeva taught the science of self-realization to his one hundred sons many thousands of years ago, as recorded in the old Sanskrit histories. The last of the *tirthankars,* Mahavir, appeared about the same time as Buddha, or five hundred years before the appearance of Lord Jesus Christ.

The Jains, who have a long tradition centering mostly upon austerity and impersonalism, are divided into two classes. These are the *swetambars* ("those who wear white"), and the *digambars* ("those who wear the directions"). The *swetambars* have facial masks that prevent them from breathing in insects, to preserve the life of even the most humble of creatures. These white-robed *munis* walk with brooms to brush insects from their path. The *digambars* wear no attire whatsoever, and eat once a day at noon only the amount of food that will fill up their two palms clasped together, this being the size of the stomach. Both groups are strictly vegetarian, and eschew all food that grows beneath the surface of the earth. I have met with the spiritual leaders of both groups at their head *ashrams,* and have had several interesting discussions, politely agreeing to disagree.

I remember once meeting a Jain gentleman on a train. The gentleman asked me "from where you are coming," and I answered "from USA."

"And you, Sir, are you from Madhya Pradesh?" I asked.

"Yes. Yes."

"Ujjain?" I asked, with the name of a nearby city.

"Yes, yes. Myself Jain."

Be that as it may, old temples attract me like a magnet. I unhesitatingly follow the narrow pathway to the temple door. I slowly put the Enfield on its side stand under a spreading *banyan* tree that appears to be several hundred years old. A few countrymen have gathered with Jain elders in front of the massive doors, greeting me as though they were expecting me. Not only do they welcome me, but also block the door, leaving me to interpret mixed signals. Now the next move will be mine, so by way of responding I remove my shoes and my belt. The strong leather belt that I bought from a policeman's uniform store in Sadar Bazar, the cantonement market, gets rolled up and placed with my shoes. The shoes were brought from America since no store in India has size 13. The crowd beams approvingly, noting that I have indeed picked up a few eastern manners during my peregrinations. Then they move aside allowing me to enter.

Smiling and nodding politely to all gathered there, I pass through the temple's palatial gateway, trying to fit in yet all the while knowing I am an oddity in their midst. Having visited thousands of Indian temples, and considering the simple architecture I estimate that this temple is from the British period, probably built in the first half of the 1800's. Beneath a tree in the courtyard lie broken stone carvings that once belonged to a vastly more ornate temple that must have stood upon this spot in centuries past. During the iconoclastic rampages of invading Moghul hordes, beautiful temples belonging to Hindus, Jains and Buddhists were razed while the resident monks attached were slaughtered wholesale. This entire region, known in ancient times as Gondwana, was overrun by the Delhi army of Akbar and was forced to bear the fury of fanatics who pummeled the peaceful local folk into submission for generations.

Within the temple compound I notice a group of men sitting pensively beneath a *bael* tree and talking softly. They rise to greet me, which gives me a chance to examine the archaeological treasures scattered about. These are ancient carvings of celestial musicians, *gandharvas,* and of their beautiful consorts the dancing *apsaras.* They are playing their stringed *vinas* and their *dholak* drums, praising God with song. These are the same universally adored angels that Christians read about in the *Bible,* since in ancient times religious teachings emanating from here in the East to the West were never restricted by passports and immigration laws. These celestial musicians or angels are not, however, situated at the highest plateau. With their instruments the *devatas* or angels celebrate and adore the One who is without a second, for He resides in the eternal world above theirs.

Angels of this Universe dwell within the upper or "heavenly" planetary systems called *swarga*. Birth in the *swarga* heavens is an elevated—but temporary—position that a man or woman of impeccable piety may hope to achieve. Although the pious get to reside there for a very long time, *swarga* nonetheless remains a material heaven within an upper planetary system, here in this physical Universe. Despite life there being more sensually fulfilling than our short spot life of a mere one hundred years here, residence in *swarga* is also temporary and subject to certain death. Like us, even these angels live in the world of planets called *mritya–loka,* place of death, wherein an embodied soul must pay for his sins or reap the temporary rewards of good deeds in his next rebirth. Like us the very breaths of the angels are precisely numbered. Unseen laws of *karma* govern these details of individual fate, which fall under the control of the leaders of the demigods like Yamaraja.

The *karma* of every individual can be read through the stars at birth. In India the science of astrology is called *jyotish,* the science of light, because it throws light upon the future. It is very ancient, and is the source of Western astrology. Only pure devotees, who have transcended the dualities of *paap* and *punya,* sin and piety, good planets and bad, make it to the other side, to the everlasting Vaikunthas, the eternal domain "where there is no fear." Lord Krishna describes all this in different ways to Arjuna on the Battlefield of Kurukshetra in the *Bhagavad-gita.*

Sitting amongst the farmers and Jain monks, I muse that anyone with a shovel could undoubtedly unearth hundreds more priceless artifacts just inches beneath our feet. A young *brahmachari* dressed in the white *dhoti* of the *swetambar* sect carefully observes me, without being obvious about it, to see if any leather remains on my person. Then he smiles gently and wordlessly directs me into the deity hall for *darshan.* There within the sanctum sanctorum two deities, marble carvings of Jain saints, sit upon the altar gazing blankly into the void of oneness. The monk identifies the first *murti* as Adi-nath. All meditating Jain *tirthankars* sitting in the *padma-asan,* or the lotus pose, appear rather similar due to their doctrine of undifferentiated monism.

I recognize the second, a 24-inch standing deity, as Bahubali. I have visited his original shrine near Mysore at the Hill of Shravanabelagola. It is said that Bahubali stood unmoving and naked in meditation upon that hill for so long that the vines and creepers of the forest entwined around his legs. There stands today a magnificent statue of him on that hill as tall as a twelve-story building. It is world famous and, despite being a religious shrine, it has become a tourist destination which attracts almost as many foreign tourists as the Taj Mahal. This is the first time I have seen a smaller version of that gigantic deity. The *brahmachari* smiles approvingly as I drop a few coins into the locked *hundi,* the donation box. It is the custom of the layman to make monetary offerings at the temples he visits for the maintenance of the temple ascetics.

Though I sometimes wonder if their extreme degree of self-deprivation is necessary, I admire the Jain ascetics. However, I do have my philosophical differences with their doctrine of absorption. These disagreements focus upon the issue of personality versus impersonality in the liberated state. But points of divergence can be saved for later as there is a technique here in the East for friendly discussion, not argument, in a civilized manner.

The Sun has traveled well past his zenith now, and will be setting soon. I need a place to sleep in a part of the world where motels and hotels do not exist. Darkness will descend and the night with its snakes, gangs of highway robbers and drunken truck drivers will make the road dangerous. My only solution is the *dharmshala,* which literally means "religious shelter." In traditional Indian fashion, the *dharmshala* provides austere lodging and simple vegetarian meals to pilgrims in return for a small donation at places of pilgrimage. The wise motorcycle pilgrim soon learns the locations of holy spots. At each of these *tirtha-bhumis* he may meet charitable souls who may offer shelter for the night. A trained eye quickly distinguishes which persons are indeed trustworthy caretakers of the *dham* from the confidence men who prey on simple tourists. In return, the pilgrim must carefully avoid offenses to holy persons and local citizens, abide by local customs, behave in a very grave and respectful manner, as well as pay the expected fees according to his means. Often I have been charged as little as ten cents for a night's stay at a *dharmshala,* and thirty cents for a square meal.

Built alongside the temple wall are several small quarters. I delicately broach the subject of staying the night. The *brahmachari* apparently likes me since I have mentioned that I am a vegetarian and have demonstrated respect and friendliness. Yes, he consents, I will be allowed to remain as a guest for the night. I thank him with folded hands, "*dhanyavad.*"

Soon, I excuse myself for a ride. Now the descending coolness of the evening air provides the most serene moments for local exploration ... to observe with wonder those facets of Indian village life that I have already seen a thousand times before, but which never cease to fascinate me. What could be nicer than this? I have no worries about where I will sleep, and before me lies an evening ride into the glorious countryside of Madhya Pradesh. Through the open gateway of the temple wall my eye drifts wistfully to the Enfield sitting stoically under the vast maze of a single *banyan* tree, one that hundreds of years ago arose from a single seed. I reflect momentarily that the bike looks quite at home here in peaceful, eternal India. Unlike cars that protrude and impose upon the landscape, the Royal Enfield motorcycle looks like it was never invented. It seems to have been here just as long as the *banyan* tree itself, which today, at least in my imagination, is forever. One swift kick and the cylinder fires up.

In the sapphire sky, colored by that moment that hangs between night and day, lingers a brilliantly waxing Moon waiting his turn to follow the east-to west path of the setting Sun. Just below the golden pearl of the Moon is the white diamond of Venus; while above this conjunction is the yellow sapphire of Jupiter. It is the meeting of celestial *brahmanas*: Jupiter or Brihaspati the priest of the gods; Venus or Shukra the *guru* of the demons; and Chandra the Moongod, lord of medicinal herbs and supplier of the juice of life. Who could put a price tag upon the blessing of this ride in this place at this time and under these stars? The Moon and his associates are freely spreading their many blessings upon everyone, never considering if the recipient is old or young, pious or impious, *shudra* or *brahman*. This night the evening *gayatri* will be chanted from behind chrome handlebars.

According to the lunar Vedic calendar, today is Shravan *shukla tritiya*, or the third day of the waxing Moon in July-August. As the Moon and his retinue enjoy their descent over the old rolling hills, a timed chorus of frogs arises in unison from the roadside marsh, amplifying with the growing darkness. As I roll back the throttle, my ears delight in hearing the thumper's beat as it crawls in harmony with twilight's orchestra. The frogs know that they are safe from hungry birds, hence their bravery now. The birds have all returned to their nests for the settled company of their mates. There is no traffic now but for me.

With the turn of the engine; the whir of the chain; the rolling tires touching the Earth; and even the rhythmic song of the mufflers; I feel myself moving in harmony with the stars above. The seven great sages, the *sapta-rishis* of the sky, who reside in the constellation of the Great Bear, lead the other stars by respectfully circumambulating the Pole Star, keeping that fixed and holy point on their right. Now that the cycle of the day has turned to night with the exit of the Sun's chariot in the West, the weather has changed. I am cloaked in the breeze of evening time.

Like night following day, India's six seasons follow one another: *vasant, ghrishma, varsha, sharad, shishir* and *hemant*. These are life-giving spring, summer, the monsoon rains, autumn, early winter and deep winter. Next follow in the grand scheme of time, the generational changes of the Earth. The thirty-year round of Saturn through the twelve rashis, or astrological signs measures these cycles. The Universe, too, has its tour of seasons that are measured in four *yuga* cycles: *satya, treta, dwapara,* and *kali yuga*. These are the ages of gold, silver, copper and iron. We are presently a little over five thousand years into the discordant iron age of *kali*, marked by widespread rancor, which lasts 432,000 years. Each *yuga* goes on for 432,000 years longer than the previous one, so the full cycle equals 432,000+864,000+1,296,000+1,728,000=4,320,000. The downward series of numbers which begins and ends the equation: 4, 3 and 2, together add up to 9 which is the perfect full number. Following 9 is the number 10, which equals 1+0=1, starting the numerical cycle over again. And indeed it does, for these *yuga* cycles continue throughout the life of our temporary universe, which is predominated by the *nava-grahas* or "nine planetary deities."

Along the roadside ahead I see a couple of still draped human forms. As the bike draws me through the sapphire night, I can make out that these are two ladies, heads and faces modestly covered with their saris. Each woman holds a *lota* of water in her right hand, and each turns her back to my lone procession as I pass. I twist back the throttle just to leave them in the dignity of attending to their evening business undisturbed and covered by the blanket of night. There is no plumbing in these villages. The fear of snakes in the fields and jackals in the forest has sent these ladies over to the roadside.

Apart from my headlamp, one solitary light bulb disturbs the music of night's descending landscape, and that is the one affixed beacon-like to the temple gate visible from far away. Following that 100-watt beacon like a moth, I find that the Jain *brahmachari* and his village associates are waiting for me by the doorway. This group of new friends, who were so casual about my departure a little over an hour earlier, has stood vigil for my safe return. Putting my faith in the best of human nature, I decide that they must have been worried for my safety on the road alone at night. Bolstered by these good thoughts, I become as happy to see each one as they are to see me. Now that I have placed my trust in them, within their temple compound. For this night at least, I shall be protected from all that is evil in this world.

In a land that is strange to him, a lone motorcyclist must learn how to tell who is to be trusted—and how far. The price of a foolish and poorly calculated friendship can be a very bitter lesson. A quick decision about where confidence should be placed is the acquired skill of a savvy wanderer. Learning this skill is the sole means of avoiding catastrophe. Any number of dropped out, would-be worldwide wanderers can be found in America or Europe. They will try to convince you that all Indians are cheats simply because they carelessly chose to befriend some Delhi train station con artist or Bombay predator. To such as these I would advise that he who abandons his homeland must not assume an air of abandon.

The Jain monk chooses this moment to introduce himself. I learn that he is a college graduate from Jabalpur. As several of his friends stand around in a half circle, he tells me of a Jain *muni* or "great thinker," who performed severe penance here over a thousand years ago. The original temple that once stood here, he says, was already several hundreds of years old when it was razed by barbaric invaders from Delhi some four centuries ago. No temple stood here for a couple of centuries, as long as the Islamic sword of intolerance was feared. With the rise of the British Raj, a new *mandir* was built thanks to the crown's more laissez-faire policy.

In unpracticed English syllables, the monk beckons me to sit. We find ourselves discussing the spiritual question of personalism versus voidism in the absolute realm. His concept is that the individual personality found here is merely an illusion and must be transcended. I agree, yet emphasize that rising above the material ego, which is based upon temporary bodily distinction, means to not become *shunya*, or devoid of personality. Rather, liberation from matter into spirit means finding the dormant and hidden spiritual identity, the eternal super-ego. He feels that a liberated soul is free of duty, whereas I profess that the real activity and function of the entity becomes awakened at the point of true enlightenment. My patience has paid off and now it is the right time to convey my point of view.

"Listen, *brahmachariji*," I insist, "I have come here upon my motorcycle, right? It needs two wheels to travel. Similarly, the two personalities, namely the subordinate individual *jiva* and the worshipful Supreme Lord of all *jivas*, are a necessary formula in the concept of personal spiritual emancipation. How many unicycles have you seen plying the Damoh Road?"

The monk has never heard of a unicycle, so the example flies over his head. Here on the other side of the world you get used to this. I mean, how much do we Westerners know about their culture, history or religion? We finish up politely enough, yet predictably in the end neither one of us convinces the other: it is a mere exercise of wits. Yet it is an important exercise because this dialogue has shown my new friends a familiarity with their culture. So, changing the topic to a more mundane one I inquire "Do you see many foreigners here?"

The crowd standing round now finds a way into joining our conversation; the previous topic was too esoteric for farmers. They deliberate the issue with great interest among themselves for a few minutes before the monk answers, "Yes, many."

"When was the last one,"

"Not long ago. Maybe six months or a year. Before that we cannot remember," he replies with an air of satisfaction.

With my Enfield as my steed, I have been to many places where a white man has not been seen in recent memory. Yet here my desire to see myself as some Columbus-like trailblazer evaporates. I never liked the courageous brute anyway.

Finally I am allowed to bring my bike into the courtyard. I wash and am offered a little *prasadam*, temple food of rice and *dal*, which is served upon a plate of dried flat leaves held together by tiny twigs. After dinner, I am shown my quarters. Hospitality, food, and shelter: here in India even those country folks who have little to offer give freely of what they have. And it is amazing just how soundly you can sleep after a day of good-weather motorcycling, for the ride is carried into your dreams.

I awaken just before sunrise as the head monk is preparing for the first *puja* of the day. The other *ashram munis* have already left for a tiny temple atop a nearby hill, a steep and penitent walk of about a mile. A bucket of unheated water and a steel *lota* are offered for my morning ablutions. Bathing takes less that ten minutes the Indian way, by pouring water over my head. Long ago necessity taught me how to bathe in public. The rule is to never become totally undressed even in bathing; instead one deftly substitutes his wet *gumcha* for dry garments simultaneously. After the *arati*, the traditional offering of a *ghee* lamp to the temple deities accompanied by the rhythmic ringing of bells, we partake of an austere breakfast together in silence.

All this reminds me of the dozen years that I too spent as a Vaishnava *brahmachari* in service to the *ashram*. Often my greatest anxiety then was that I might someday leave. Yet somehow nothing has really changed, only the externals differ. I am still the same soul struggling for inner realization. And while the rotating externals pass me by, I try to remain indifferent to the insensitive gyrations of the world as heat and cold, pain and happiness, wealth and poverty pass before me. Each rising and setting Sun leaves the body a day older and nearer to the appointed time on the calendar. But here and now I am a rolling pilgrim in an ancient land, savoring eternal truths on a timeless quest, and on two wheels, too. What more could be asked for?

The lead ascetic and a few village men stand around politely as Old Reliable cranks over on the first kick. While it is still early, I need to make a break, to merge with the road. Even if the temperature stays in the 70's, the Sun will still turn brutal after passing the noon zenith. In India it is said that the morning Sun gives energy while the afternoon Sun depletes it. That is why the Indian *pandits* and astrologers refer to the Sun as a *krura* or cruel planet. The other planets of Vedic *jyotish* or astrology are either *shubhas* (benefics) or *paapis* (malefics). But the Sun has a touch of both, like fire that cooks our food yet burns our fingers if we get too close. Indeed the entire schedule of India is adapted to this solar principal. Most Indians take their midday meal around one o'clock, then rest for an hour or two away from the Sun. But they are not lazy: they make up for it by working late. During the hours of late day when the Sun's rays are cruel, only "mad dogs and Englishmen" will venture out. It is not uncommon to walk into a store in the bazaar during the afternoon only to find the owner stretched out on a straw mat. He knows that shoppers will reappear in the evening hours.

My morning ride is refreshing. With the help of the early Sun's benefic rays, my mind can reflect upon life's secret mysteries ... and upon the Hands that pull the strings. The easy rolling motion of the wheels directs the motorcycle pilgrim to see himself in the puzzle of the changing wheel of life. I know from experience that moto-meditation will be difficult later when the rays become like flaming needles. When the mind is boiling and on the verge of sunstroke, the ability to calculate split second movements so necessary for road survival will be compromised. Starry solar flashes blur the vision causing blind spots that can hide oncoming vehicles. The instinct for survival demands that the moto-*yogi* guard himself from the torment caused by baking in the afternoon rays. An early start is a good one.

Listening to the purposeful resonation of the engine, I reflect that this bike is built from the inside out and from the rocky road up. It has been created from a noble British heritage, and is produced today by Indians for India, which pretty much means that it can cover any worldwide condition. The Royal Enfield Company began in the 19th century by making cannons and small arms in England. Their first motorcycle appeared just after the turn of the twentieth century, and Royal Enfield—like Norton, Triumph, BSA and Matchless—eventually became a top marque. Royal Enfield motorcycles won many races and supported the British military in two wars, as they support the Indian Army to this day.

The single-cylinder Bullet model that I ride was developed in the late forties, and built in England until the mid-fifties. When operations wound down in England in 1955, India bought the tooling. Royal Enfield production transferred to Madras, now Chennai, where the same half-century old technology has been churning out the same bikes year after year. If there ever was a "if it isn't broken, then don't fix it" philosophy in action then this is it. The Indians have left the design alone, and have only tightened up any weak spots. The India-built Royal Enfield is a neo-classic for adventure touring, a trail bike, and a sub-continental big cruiser. It is reliable, sturdy, secure and fit. Like wisdom, it is a faithful friend on the road. Adventure riders have taken India's Enfield from the Arctic Circle to Antarctica, and all the way around the world. In a fine and old tradition, India's military uses the machine in blazing desert sands, and in snowy Himalayan outposts. The *Guinness Book of Records* says that the maximum number of people to ride a single motorcycle formation was the Indian Army at Jabalpur, and they did it balancing on Enfields.

Being neither a stunt rider nor a trick rider; simply negotiating the most dangerous roads in the world is daring enough for me. Back in America, I have watched with awe as motorcycle racers lean into corners defying every law of nature that the common man holds true, only to switch back the other way knees scraping the ground into the next S-turn. I did try some improvisational mud jumping with the Enfield once and, misjudging my take-off, landed in a shallow monsoon lake. Indians who were not accustomed to a foreigner showing off by playing Evel Kneivel had gathered around to watch a white man make a fool of himself. When I landed in the water, the Indians turned from a giggling audience to my salvation. To my surprise the Enfield kept humming in two feet of water. By riding the tough clutch hard and with two men wading in to push, I was quickly extricated from the mud. That ended my career as a daredevil.

Many daredevil foreigners do come to India and Nepal to take mammoth hikes in the mountain wilderness, bike the Himalayan high roads into Tibet, or raft the white waters. Inevitably a few self-patronizing friendships with smiling natives begging for green cards are formed. Then it's off to Calcutta to perform their obligatory white man's burden form of charity for a few days. If they survive, and some do not, they've earned their feel-good bragging rights back home in the manicured suburbia of the West. Yet that pilgrim who wishes his heart to beat in synch with the very heartbeat of the Motherland of All Culture must take it low and slow. For me this means disappearing into my own practice of Enfield *yoga*. There are mountains to climb other than the geophysical ones. The mountain of Indian thought looms far above even Everest's highest peak.

Still, India's roads will eventually bring out the racer and the off-road scrambler, the mud rider and the dirt tracker, the cocksure adventurer who feels like a winner just by surviving. In tranquil valleys of the idyllic countryside where roads are either hardened mud or have been recently paved by tribal cliques, riding is done as much as with the hands and body as with the breath. This is the trance of *samadhi* steering. But it is when you find yourself on roads that are neither asphalt nor baked brick-hard dirt that a degree of skill is required. Roads that were once paved yet now through neglect have turned into gauntlets of old asphalt stalagmites make the road *yogi* a fierce competitor just as a matter of survival. You are likely to run into heavy traffic at times even on the worst and most remote country roads. At such times the reflexes needed to negotiate the slalom of India's pitiful highways will be all that lies between you and infinity. Falling off the bike is the motorcyclist's greatest fear. For the *yogi*, falling into a lower species of life wherein self-realization is not an option is the greatest fear. The motorcycle *yogi* defeats fear through his faith in the Yogeshwar.

Much of what was once the road to Damoh has long since disintegrated from merely a pothole infested lane to an endless path of teeth-rattling craters. The primary layer of fist-sized gravel has been beaten back up to the surface. Tire harassing rocks aimlessly bounce in every direction like window shoppers gawking at some Calcutta bazaar. To make it worse, speed bumps on Indian roads are often all that remains of a gauntlet that is nothing but a series of speed bumps. Mysterious holes dug several feet deep beside the roads are common, sitting patiently like traps-cum-future-gravesites for the unwary two-wheeler. Dunlop tires take the Rubicon challenge well, for the Indian rubber industry has risen to the occasion. Surprisingly, flat tires are relatively rare, and if your tire does deflate, there will always be some local genius around who can patch it.

It is said that that one-quarter of the world's engineers are Indians, and sometimes I think that the lanes of this land must be responsible. The roads themselves are mostly old cow trails that have evolved into by-ways that were turned into engineering disasters both by design and by neglect. The way in which the citizens that ply these roads negotiate them is another engineering marvel. This is the only country in the world where you can get pedestrian traffic jams, and the only way to face India's roads is to adopt an Indian mentality. You can forget whatever concept you've carried regarding right from wrong since birth; you are now swimming in a sea of humanity, balancing on two wheels spinning like a gyroscope. You are steering, rocking, leaning, wiggling, twisting and sliding only inches from thousands of others doing the same. This is the Great Road Microcosm reflecting God's Great Macrocosm—the divine universal marvel of engineering brought down to earth for each rider of Hindustan to behold and contemplate. Road inspiration has enlightened hordes of Indian engineers who now congregate in all corners on earth. For the foreigner who somehow still believes in signals, yellow lines that divide traffic, stop signs, highway maintenance, courtesy and a standard body of rules, life will be all too short. In the West everyone can count upon fifteen minutes of fame. However, on these roads it is hard to foresee fifteen minutes of life.

Astronomers theorize that even if different clusters of stars were to pass through each other, there would be little chance of collision. In a nutshell, this is the wonder of the Universe at work, one that reflects most accurately India's roadways most accurately. One lane's width often equals only the width of a truck, yet the road gets subdivided into as many lanes as dogs, pedestrians, rickshaws, bicycles, mopeds and motorcycles can run side by side, the direction they face being arbitrary. Vehicles and goats enter the roads without stopping like sudden meteors shooting against the established order. As they merge into the pulsating jet stream of traffic they are quickly gulped down by infinity.

Vehicle contact is actually relatively rare. Through it all, the Indian rider carries upon his face an otherworldly and detached *samadhi*-like demeanor, an expression that is a certain trademark of this land of *yoga*. As I bite the bullet and sternly gun my Enfield through some traffic snarl, at times it seems to me that any Indian could write the future bestseller *How to Get Nearly Crushed to Death Without Changing Your Facial Expression*.

The menacing looks and gestures that form the American driving ethic are simply considered bad manners around here. Sometimes it appears as though in India it is OK to nearly kill someone providing you stay calm and poised while doing it. Tolerance is The Way. Like the harsh *tapasya* of ascetic *yogis*, indifference to the sometimes miserable, hot, dusty, smoky, crowded, unkempt conditions of India's roadways can awaken higher realizations of man and his place in the cosmos. If highways as those in America were ever to get built in India, then a hundred years of road *yoga* would go down the drain as the Ayyengars; Chaterjees and Sharmas motor off to their favorite fast food hang outs or drive-through wedding chapels.

Besides, how else can you find yourself riding these country roads except by passing through the bazaars? The changing seasons of change like the cycles of the Moon god above rotate quickly before the motorcycle *yogi* in India. He must stay in touch with the inner explosive piston-propelling force of the *atma* all the while navigating through the passing parade of external attraction and repulsion like the alternating cycles of intake and exhaust. Ultimately, whether the ride takes us into a man-made hell hole or through glorious nature in all ten directions–the eight points of the compass plus up and down–the conclusion which must eventually be arrived at is this: all that we see is nothing more than the many illusory faces of the goddess of *maya*. Where will we be when those faces we hold as real melt into the earth or vaporize into the clouds?

We struggle for survival in a world wherein the basic principal of *jiva jiva sa jivanam* reigns supreme. This rule of Nature means that no living thing can survive without eating another entity, moving or non-moving. The superior entity exists only through the unwilling sacrifice of the inferior. No being invites another to come on over and eat him except cartoon farm animals on American TV ham and chicken commercials. Living at the top of the food chain like an omnivore for the sake of devouring all those below is no assurance that we will not be next. This is the relative world, Bubba, and for the here and now no one person's perch is absolute, be he the President or the Pope. Neither can we say with smug assurance to which unwilling level of the food chain we will find ourselves assigned in the next go-round.

Within the spectacular woodlands all about me the animals follow the principle of survival to the letter. Only man parading mere inches from the giant wheels of the juggernaut foolishly thinks that he is invincible. Even the very trees lending us shade in the selflessness of their spreading boughs grow and survive from a very soil whose recipe has been spiced by thousands of bodies, the collective rot of which has nourished the forest over the millennia. The dwellers of the forests say that the trees, too, know when the woodsman is sharpening his axe.

The *Bhagavad-gita* says that this natural beauty is neither false, nor is it an illusion, yet all this is temporary. Lord Krishna informs Arjuna that this world is a personal, yet material, reflection of the original and personal spiritual world. That which is reflected has its origin in that which is original. Without the prototype, the copy could not exist. The reflection or secondary is as real as the original for it too has been generated. However this world of reflections or *maya* should not be mistaken to be the primary. He who finds himself bewildered by the reflection should consider seeking out the original, lest he become lost in a continuous maze of reflections of the reflections. The net is never-ending, Bubba. But he who has been empowered with the sword of knowledge to cut through this web of reflective illusions is he who can hope to discover the original. He who is entangled in the image cannot be relied upon as a proper leader to guide us who are confounded by the question of reality versus reflective-reality. Who will lead us to that place which is beyond the forest of illusion? That *yogi* who is qualified is the *guru*, the *nayaka*, the *acharya*, and the spiritual master. He is the self-realized devotee of the Supreme Absolute Truth who acts as the eyes of the struggling seeker. He is both easy and impossible to find. Discovering the qualified *guru* depends entirely upon the willingness of he who seeks to surrender.

My *guru* is as deep as the ocean, or rather even the ocean becomes shallow before his munificence. Today I am astride my Enfield in the bliss of motorcycle *yoga* carrying the Name of God by his grace. We have but little time upon this earth and the foremost mission is the supreme self-knowledge that propels us back to our original position. Achievement of the eternal platform from which rebirth is never a possibility is the true goal of all *yoga, karma, hatha, ashtanga, jnana,* or motorcycle.

Lord Krishna informs Arjuna that this world is one of many personal yet material reflections of the one personal yet spiritual world. In the One there are many, and many find their refuge in the One. In other words, the material Universe with its finite-in-number and all-too-temporary planets is a reflection of the spiritual Universe with its infinite and unfathomable eternal spiritual planets inhabited by liberated souls. They who dwell in the liberated state are cognizant of the Yogeshwar. The unfettered *bhakta*, liberated through loving service to the Lord, is the *yogi* who has crossed the finish line. He alone knows the Yogeshwar, the master of all mysticism. This is the final word of the *Bhagavad-gita*: *yatra yogeshwar krishna*. Liberation also awaits the moto-*yogi* that has become a rider in that fuel-enriched school whose explosive all-propelling petrol is the holy name of God.

Soon my occasionally transcendental thoughts are interrupted by a huge shadow blowing over from the West. From behind me, a fast moving rider glued to his two-stroke Rajdoot—and wearing a cinema hero's pencil-thin mustache on his detached-looking face, zigzags around me. He indifferently passes me within inches though the road is empty. Noting that he is drenched, I realize that he is outrunning an approaching storm. As giant drops begin to sacrifice themselves onto dry earth all around me, tiny wisps of dust rise up from delicate crater-like impressions. Since early monsoon storm systems can be very localized, I decide to race the cloud. As the tap tap tap of the rain god Indra's handiwork becomes audible, I must make a decision. While the dark blue cloud pours itself into oblivion onto some grateful farmer's field I gun the throttle pushing onward.

Another two miles and there appears off to my right an old temple upon an older hillock that has been brightly festooned with banners. The sharp rhythmic beat of the wooden *dholak* drum echoing across the road accompanied by the wail of reed horns is irresistible. The joyous sound of the music bouncing from hill to hill beckons each villager to attend, and I am not one to refuse an invitation. Today is *naag-paanchami*, the fifth day of the waxing Moon in the Vedic month of Shravan, a day when simple villagers perform *puja* to India's most deadly residents, her cobras. As I wend the bike down through the maze of unknown lanes like one hypnotized, the sounds of celebration grows louder. The temple sits proudly atop the hill guarding the Damoh Road and its wayfarers as though it has been there since time immemorial. For a deja-vu moment it seems as though I too have always been here: I am transformed from an eternal stranger now home at last by the smiles of the snake worshippers. The bike gets parked beside a few others, mostly old two-strokes and step-throughs.

A large crowd of simple villagers and a few separate groups of tribals huddling on their haunches are watching a snake charmer's show. Today is one of the very few days of the year when he can make a little money: this is his window and he knows it. From a demographic perspective, his job is probably among the world's worst career choices. Recently a *National Geographic* film crew followed a snake charmer from Govardhan to Delhi. The documentary noted that in the nation's capitol there is hardly enough interest for him to earn his meager bus fare. India wants to lope along into the 21st century and the snake charmer has become the unwitting symbol of all that stands for Third World superstition and backwardness. Not only that, but animal rights activists have made him a target by forming a sort of impromptu serpent liberation front, forcibly seizing snakes from the circular straw basket of the charmer. The snake charmers wonder: at least my snake gets to eat, why don't the do-gooders just go adopt all the stray dogs?

The simple design of the white washed temple suggests that it is a little over one hundred years old. Asking locals a temple's age will inevitably yield the same answer, "*Bahut purana, Sahib*" or "It is very old, Sir," So I rely on my own crude methods of trying to date them based upon architecture and other clues. Inside there is an older Shiva-*linga* which, having received festive prayers, is adorned with red hibiscus flowers and has been bathed with milk. Upon the large black *linga* the village *brahman* has drawn three parallel lines with sandalwood paste, the *tilak* of Shiva's followers representing horizontal or material expansion. A *ghee* lamp's five cotton wicks still smolder before the great god showing that the *puja* was completed just moments before my arrival. *Ghee*-rich smoke from the fire *yagna* still hangs in the air. I feel in my pocket for a rupee note and pull out a fifty. All eyes are on me and I do not wish to appear miserly. Nor do I want to reveal how much money I have, so the fifty gets offered beside the incense. I bow down among the lingering prayers of a hundred simple supplicants, and the devotion is heavy.

The *Puranas* tell how once upon a time Lord Shiva dutifully drank some poison that otherwise would have caused the destruction of the world. As the great god lifted this deadly potion called *hala-hala* to his lips, some drops fell to the ground. Serpents licked it up and from that time onward became venomous. Therefore snake festivals are always associated with Lord Shiva who wears a cobra, a *naag*, as a garland. During my travels I have also visited a few rare temples of the snake god himself, like the Vasukinath *mandir* in Prayag or the Sangameshwar Temple on the Naag River, and imagine for a moment that today there must be a gala festival at those places, too.

I offer my respects to Shiva who is known by a variety of names. Because the Moon god rests as a decoration within his dark locks, he is called Chandrashekhar, "he who keeps the Moon as an ornament." Due to the spot of poison on his otherwise golden throat, he is called Nilkant, "he whose throat is blue." After the Ganges came crashing down from *swarga* or heaven onto his head, he came to be known as Gangadhar. He is considered the "greatest of the demigods." or *devatas*, and hence is called Mahadeva. He lives as an ascetic in a remote Himalayan region and is known as Kailashpati, "the lord of Mt. Kailash." He is Parvatinath, "husband of the goddess whose father rules the *parvat* or mountain." With his fiery third eye he is Trinayana. He is Trishuladhar, carrier of the trident. The great god is the lord, or *ish*, of the serpents and thus is called *naaga-ish* which combines to form "Naagesh." These very old Vedic concepts of Shiva-worship quite understandably left British Christian missionaries vexed, but no amount of foreign coercion could decelerate Hindustan's love of Lord Shiva.

At a roadside temple of Nagesh, Shiva, the lord of cobras

Mantras said, I leave the temple to sit among the celebrants. However, mingling is not all that easy in a place where many have never seen a foreigner. A crowd of young men quickly gathers around me grinning and bobbing their heads. Uneasily I return their looks trying to show no nervousness, despite my obvious numerical disadvantage. With folded hands and a sort of warped grin I fold my hands and say *"namaste."*

Having had this kind of attention before, I am well aware that unfriendly or fearful body language can be very hazardous to one's health. But this rustic group redefines intimate; they roll up my pants to see what a blonde white man's leg hairs look like. Dozens of inquisitive brown hands glide over my shins. I know that this is not merely good-natured fun, they are also daring me to react, and if I don't pass their little acid test I could be ground into snake food. Eventually I rise slowly and back away to the bike, grinning at them as they grin at me. I feel I have won them over and any one of them at this point would give up his day's meal if I were to announce that I am hungry. But on second thought I wouldn't bet on it. Besides I am less of a gambling man than a traveling man, and the Enfield beckons.

After making sure that the bike will fire, I shout "Har Har Mahadeva," as sort of my own "Hi Ho Silver." Each person in this all-male crowd responds jubilantly with hands waving in the air, responding with "Har Har Mahadeva." I wend my way down the maze of paths that lead out of this tiny village, the name of which I still do not know. Ladies walking along the hard dirt roadway turn their heads away and resist the temptation of even giving a glance to a member of a race they have only heard of. Chastity is the supreme quality of the Hindu woman. The legendary shyness and modesty to which she is heir is the very quality upon which all other facets of Hindu culture and religion rests. It has been rightly said that no object of veneration occupies a more noble position than one's mother ... and to the saint all women are his mothers.

The remaining hour or so that it takes to get to Damoh proves to be a glorious ride as expected. The early start is to be thanked. Damoh, I will find, is a town of approximately 100,000 people. The biggest industry here is the *bidi*, the cheap, hand-rolled, lung burning, string-tied, horn-shaped, smelly, little brown cigarettes that kills millions of addicted peasant men who smoke together in roadside huddles. The town of Damoh is the headquarters for Damoh District, which is comprised of about five smaller towns and 1400 villages with a total population of around 900,000. In a place such as this, wherein half the people know neither the Hindi nor English alphabet, optometrists make patients read eye charts depicting smaller and larger images.

From Damoh, the middle of nowhere cannot even be seen, yet as I enter the town I find a satisfied self-sufficiency about the place. It moves at its own pace, and is nothing more or less than what I had expected it to be. Riding from street to street I realize that when all the Earth's big cities are leveled, Damoh is the sort of place that will always be here, come flood or nuclear holocaust. Bare electric wires dangling from a power pole throw sparks inches above the heads of nonchalant passers-by. Bizarre scooter-powered goods carriers with seven wheels wobble down lanes with bicyclists hanging on the rear for a free ride. Seven men dressed in orange *dhotis* in imitation of *sadhus* are marching a huge and noble elephant through town. Here, just like every other place in India, lesser beings who walk must fatalistically accept that anyone who has a car "has permission" to jeopardize the pedestrian's life. It is frustrating and useless, yet tempting, to make the natural comparisons: if this were America everyone driving would be thrown in jail.

After *darshan*, or "seeing" the deity, at a locally celebrated Shiva temple, I relax upon the *ghera* platform that has been built under a *bael* tree. Bael trees are considered sacred, and ladies seeking longevity for their husbands have wrapped this one with red strings. Probably the number one prayer among Hindu wives is to never face widowhood, since they fear being swept aside by upcoming generations with no one to look out for them. Those who do outlive their husbands often choose to spend their impoverished last days in widows' ashrams of Vrindavan or Varanasi.

For fifteen rupees, about thirty cents, I purchase six bananas and three mangoes from the *phal-walla* pushing his wooden cart, and can now enjoy a satisfying lunch. Some locals have been observing me politely, out of the corner of their eyes, though pretending not to. In the big cities like Calcutta strangers will gladly interrupt your lunch to pound and bait you with puerile questions, but here in Madhya Pradesh it is different. These people, though unsophisticated, have manners and dignity.

A Mr. Gupta, who has patiently waited for me finish my repast, now approaches. As we chat, he narrates a very funny episode. Yesterday he had met a group of village pilgrims who had come to Damoh hoping to witness a miracle. On the outskirts of town, there is a pair of temples side by side, one for Shiva and the other for his spouse Parvati. The pilgrims had somehow heard that when these two temples come together, a gala wedding ceremony would be performed for the divine couple to celebrate the miracle. However, they were a little disappointed because what actually occurred was that the two temple flags had become entwined due to a sudden shift in the wind. The mere combining of the two flags had let loose a volley of rumors.

Sitting under the *bael* tree, I notice a small seedling that has struggled to life between cement cracks in the ghera. This is a plant sowed by no hand of man; neither does anyone tend to it daily. This plant reaching upward against all hope reminds me of a seedling that my guru maharaja once pointed to in New York City, growing from the cracks of the sidewalk on the Lower East Side. He mentioned that denizens of heaven, their pious assets exhausted, return to Earth to begin their journey again through 8,400,000 species of life from the bottom up. For the student *yogi*, even the guru's casual, off-handed comments are as good as scripture.

Resuming my ride around Damoh, I come upon an unusual sight. A troupe of over two dozen *hijras*, or eunuchs, are dancing and singing in and around the apartment house of a newborn boy. Superstition says that if they are not adequately compensated, a figure that can set a gainfully employed father back a two-week's salary, then the baby will bear the eunuchs' curse for life. The *hijras* are one group of entertainers that no one pays to arrive; they are paid to leave.

India's hijras, castrated men, dance at weddings and birth ceremonies. That wise fellow on the far left is the guru.

Above doorways in the narrow lanes, the entrances to apartments bear markings of house blessings: the auspicious red symbols and *yantras* drawn there by pandits with bright red *kum kum* powder mixed with *ghee*. India is the only place on Earth where the *swastika* and the Star of David sit side by side as religious emblems, innocently oblivious of any other connotation beyond Hinduism. The Star of David to the Hindus is the ancient Lakshmi *yantra*. Like the yin-yang symbol of the universe, the downward triangle represents the female principle and the upward triangle or *trikona* represents the male energy. Meditation upon this yantra carries the thoughtful *yogi* from the material and embodied concept of male-female, to the diverse energies of the spiritual world, ultimately culminating in Shri Radha-Krishna. The enjoyer-enjoyed concept remains even in absolute transcendence. The *swastika* is used by Hindus to invoke all that is auspicious. Unfortunately, it was ripped off from India by the Nazis, and misused as a symbol of hatred and false supremacy.

As red as each *yantra*, are the splatters of dried paan spittle on walls outside doorways. These have been deposited by neighbors visiting neighbors. Alternating smells of incense and horse dung, cooked spices and exhaust fumes, tantalize and torture the senses. All around are the usual small town establishments, some with signs that read: "Beauty Saloon," "Homely Cooking Restaurant," "Departmental Store" or "Meals Hotal."

An overturned pedal *ricksha*, clumsily overloaded, has caused a minor traffic jam in the very narrow lane. In front of me a nifty econo-box, the Tata Indica, tries to back into me. This particular car has an electronic back-up warning system that plays "Jingle Bells." The irony that this is a Hindu country and Christmas was six months ago is apparently lost upon the driver who is trying to run me over in reverse. Noticing that the *ricksha-wala* has righted his rig, the car stops reversing. As I maneuver around the car, I somehow recall a cycle ricksha driver that I rode with twenty years earlier in Lucknow. He was bragging that talent scouts from the Bombay film industry had noticed his daughter's natural abilities, and had offered her a film role with some of the day's leading ladies. To tide him over a bit, until the talent scouts called him to Bombay, they gave him five hundred rupees, and took his daughter. The simple *ricksha-wala* did not realize that he has been tricked into selling his daughter into prostitution.

Soon the time comes to search for a clean hotel. Finding accommodations will not be difficult, but locating a reasonably clean lodging can be a real conundrum. The problem lies at the root of India's top-heavy class structure and is a snarled little socio-economic problem to unravel. The lowest rung on the ladder is the *shudra* or working caste, yet still lower than they are the *bungis*, the toilet cleaners. No uppercasteman wishes to be known as a toilet cleaner, so rather than clean his hotel himself, the hotel owner brings in the *bungis*. The *bungis* are a wretched lot, miserably underpaid, and as a result quite naturally take no pride in their work. Consequently toilets can go beyond reeking, they can broil your nose with toxic ammonia fumes. In a hot country where almost everything that is drunk down becomes perspiration, any liquids that pass out naturally are rather distilled. Some toilets could literally make you faint from the obnoxious fumes, and at times I've really feared falling victim to TDS, toilet death syndrome. Ordinary intelligence would dictate being a little bit more generous toward the *bungis*. At least here and now in the India of *kali yuga*, it is a place for transcendental philosophy, and not common sense.

Finally I find a reasonably decent hotel with not only clean toilets but also a strong fan above the bed. Better fans in India rotate 1,000 times a minute and create a wind that is powerful enough to blow away the dreaded malaria-carrying mosquitoes that appear at sunset. The wise traveler soon learns in the interest of survival to discern the cheap fans from the good ones. I have estimated that a mosquito can at bed level enter a wind current created by a ceiling fan blowing up to eight hundred times a minute, but at around one thousand rpm's the frustrated little bloodsucker, try as he might, is blown away.

I once came down with malaria in Sitapur on my way to Naimisharanya up north in U.P. I lay burning with a 105 degree fever for a week next to an outside garbage pile infested with millions of biting, buzzing insects, where my pious Hindu host had dumped me. When I would come out of my shakes and delirium to beg squatting, staring peasants to go get me medical help; they would tell me that it was "too far," or "out of their way". "*Bahut dur, sahib.*" The experience cured me of any illusions regarding the hospitality all Indians claim they have, for jewels are not to be found in every mountain, nor pearls in every oyster.

Eventually the jewels and pearls found me. *Vaishnava sadhus*, holy monks, from the Gaudiya Math in nearby Naimisharanya, took me in. The doctor they summoned visited me twice daily. Arriving by bicycle, he gave me quinine injections each morning and herbal *ayurvedic* ("life-knowledge") supplements in the evening. For these fourteen visits plus medicine I was billed ninety rupees, which was about ten dollars at that time. After a week, a *sadhu* came in to show me a peacock outside the door with his feathers in full fan. That was an omen telling me that I would recover. A week earlier I had made out from the doctor's Hindi, as he spoke with the *sadhus*, that I might shake my way into my next life. I'll never forget the doctor's look of compassion now that he was telling me with a casual wave of his hand, *bimar hogya*: "Your sickness is gone."

To this day I owe my life to that doctor and the Gaudiya Math *sadhus*, although I remain wary of mosquitoes. If biting bugs come too close, I am merciless. My Jain friends are taught to tolerate them, fearing next-life retribution. However, this is another albeit minor point of philosophical disagreement, for my tolerance must run out when survival is threatened. I follow that school of *yoga* that dictates, "The highest goal is to save yourself, for he who is trapped in a well cannot help others trapped with him to escape."

Looking back, I remember an early introduction to the basic scripture of yoga, the *Bhagavad Gita*, thirty-five years ago. It was the sixties in Haight Ashbury, and the edition I carried with me was not very carefully translated, hence I drew many incorrect conclusions. I imagined that soon I would be able to discover my own Lordship over the Universe, my Universal Form, when I would become God. Later my Guru Maharaj advised me to become like Arjuna and work for the satisfaction of the Yogeshwar rather than trying to become the Yogeshwar.

That evening in my hotel room reading those same verses again, only now with a deeper understanding, I doze off under the fan. On the Battlefield of Kurukshetra, at the start of the Great War, Arjuna has just witnessed the Universal Form of Yogeshwar Shri Krishna. Realizing the supreme potency of the Lord of the Worlds, Arjuna begs to be pardoned for any offense he may have caused "in friendship or in love." Sleep that night after a long slow ride is deep and delicious, the kind you drink in gulps. I have yet to understand the level of those maha-*yogis* who have renounced even sleep, like my own guru maharaj.

The next day I awaken refreshed to the mantric chanting of the Hindi *Ramayana* of Tulsidas. The all-auspicious blowing of a temple conch shell, the sound of which gives flight to all evils, enters my room from some nearby temple. After bathing, I apply coconut oil to my face as protection from the wind on my day's ride. Coconut oil is also my thermometer because it solidifies into a cream at around sixty-seven degrees and becomes liquid above that. Hence it is a lazy man's thermometer, one that reads either hot or cool. Sailors used to look forward to India as a land where they would find a tree that provided both a meal and a drink. And skin lotion, too. The hotel owner, Mr. Agarwal, spots my open door and peeks in to invite me to his home behind the hotel. We walk through a garden-like courtyard and enter his drawing room.

The obligatory black and white photos of departed relatives are hung upon the walls. They gaze downward from dusty frames, each with the serious expression of one who is trying to get the punchline of a joke he just cannot understand. Somewhere in India there must be a School of Photography for the Soon-to-be Deceased that teaches the subject how to make this quizzical face. The photographer is taught how to tell a joke with no punch line and while the subject struggles with its meaning, he clicks the shutter. This could be the only explanation for millions of photos in homes all over India with the same facial expression. The art of mortuary photography means telling a joke that the subject gets only when he dies. The punch line is that you have struggled so hard your entire life, yet all that is left to remember you by is a black and white likeness of yourself gazing down from the wall. Each photo could be captioned "You're next." This is a bad joke written by the goddess of illusion, and is why the moto-*yogi* has a throttle to twist and a credo that states "just ride away." Yet unless the holy name is the vehicle, this joke of no laughter will be repeated. Though the god of death Yama is patient, he has no dearth of work.

To my pleasant surprise as Mr. Agarwal sits me down, the television goes off. In many homes nowadays they will raise the volume to intrude over your conversation. When I first came to India in the 1970's there was only one channel called Doordarshan, or "that which is exceptional to behold," and no color TV. I did not see a color television until 1981. At the houses of the rich, thirty or forty members of the working class would huddle quietly on the seth's porch and peer in to see the dim TV through a screen door. My first glimpse of an Indian TV show was pudgy Indian actors showing off their overstuffed handsomeness, starchly dressed as cowboys and enjoying a saloon brawl in the Wild West. Today, thanks to the ubiquitous television, the final threads of the social fabric of a once great India have been nearly unraveled. Vile Hollywood-style degradation has been invited into every home, ancient India's refined art, culture, dance and theater have all turned south taking morality down the tubes—yes, pun intended—in the wake of music videos. Not only that, but a huge portion of the products advertised nationally are actually manufactured by American companies which have displaced many really decent indigenous products. Today many locally owned companies have been bought out by American corporations, who simply phase them out in favor of Western brand names. Remember the Lay's potato chip "Betcha can't eat just one" ad? You guessed it. Thirty-five years later this ad has finally arrived in India with predictable success.

In the 1970's the Indian government demanded the formula for Coca-Cola, at that time a bottle of which cost a rupee and a half. When Coke refused to divulge, the Indian government ordered the shutdown of their factory. An indigenous cola—and quite a good one—called Thum's Up was formulated to replace Coke. Today Coke is back and is so ubiquitous, it is as though it never left. And you guessed it, Thum's Up, which has it's own motto "I want my thunder," is owned by Coca-Cola. So whether you want your thunder or not, getting away from the exploitation of first-worldism gets harder every day, even on a motorcycle in Damoh. Not to say that you can't discover some really great indigenous products like Neem toothpaste made from the astringent *nim* tree. Or *chyavan prash*, the ayurvedic tonic that can boost sexual strength and clear out the lungs. Or *sari bada salsa* which cleans the blood and the urinary tract. From coconut oil to sandalwood soap to *kalmegh* for the liver, India's list of ancient gifts goes on despite the glare of Western commercialism that blinds the new generation.

Recently a hundred and fifty Michael Jackson "look-alikes" and thousands of fans, rioted in Delhi when the idol did not show up "as promised," as if anyone really had invited the mega-star. Nonetheless, today young hopefuls in every Indian film imitate the Moonwalker's vulgar dance, crass moves that would make a lambada dance teacher blush. Once culturally rich periodicals graced every newsstand, but now all those literate journals have all been replaced by TV and film gossip tabloids. Rags that celebrate Bollywood careers that are born with one issue and, like the stars they tattle on, are tossed out before the next month's issue hits the stands. You tell me, will Mungphalli ever marry Mirchi now that his little tryst with socialite Zhareefer Batliwalli has been discovered? In India toilet paper never caught on, since it has been proven to cause berrius-dinglitis, yet filmy magazines have filled the void.

The hot milk spiced with cardamom, saffron and ginger served by Mrs.

Agarwal is refreshing. The entire family is pious and beautiful, and even the usual questions become a source of joyful exchange without the distraction of television. I wonder how the Agarwals survive running a hotel in an unheard of place like Damoh. Yet Mr. Agarwal is quite wealthy. In our casual conversation I am surprised to learn that he has a son who has settled in Calgary. When he tells me how smart and honest we Americans are, I realize that their concept of us falls short as ours of them. Not only is India 180 degrees from America in terms of physical location, but everything else is quite different as well. Damoh is not for the traveler who wants quasi-Americana waiting for him wherever he gets off the plane. Damoh is for the curious adventurer who prefers to see a place on Earth which least resembles that place he calls home.

Desiring to take leave of the Agarwals while morning the Sun is still giving energy, I request their kind permission to go. This is done with a particular look conveying that the moment for departure has arrived. Politeness demands that this look must be communicated at the right time, which means when the teacups are empty. For a Westerner, this look is an acquired art, yet an essential one, because it can save you from quite a bit of monotonous and routine conversation. After all, a visit to India is not for talking about America; it is for getting away from America. Immediately, I receive the answer from Mr. Agarwal in a moment's returned glance that permission is granted, and his family in unison with their head respectfully rises to see me off. All the members of the cultured Agarwal family escort me out to the bike. TV show be damned, each one stands there until I have left. The guest is god at the Agarwal's: *atithi devo bhava*. Before me sits the world's most beautiful sight, my Enfield, since it is morning time and I am in the mood to ride.

Waving good-bye to them, the feeling of love I harbor for not only the Agarwal family and their ancestors, but for a million other honest souls struggling here in this vast strange country, is undeniable. Somehow people in India eke out a living against all odds in an environment that makes America's poor quite rich by comparison. Against all odds the faithful are preserving their ancient heritage and extending the world's oldest culture into the future. Many times *pandits* have explained to me that only certain souls with the unseen asset of past-life piety—*purva-punya phal*—may be born here. Only an inborn and inbred faith in God preserves the Hindu's dharma in Vedic India. Toil he must, yet according to his fate he stoically faces his due suffering or accepts his reward. God alone decides the result, and His final edict is accepted unquestioningly. Besides, whatever happens here is temporary, and in the future a better place awaits the faithful.

Riding through the bazaars of Damoh, the city seems much the same as the one that welcomed me the previous evening. Except it is the early morning now and the sweepers are expected to single-handedly push back the tsunami tide of rubbish that has been thrown down by insensitive hands. On my left a frail old lady sweeper, whose father was a sweeper and whose children and grandchildren will all die as sweepers, pushes with her straw *jharu* several layers of garbage into a huge mountain. Young men with nothing to do stand about indifferently chewing *paan*.

Around town I notice a couple of old missionary schools. After independence, the British went back to their foggy islands leaving the work of conversion to the converts. The Christian missionary's job was to subvert Hindu society from the bottom by telling the sweepers and other "*dalits*" that if they were to convert, then they would become "equal". However, after conversion, many sweepers were disappointed to find that they were expected to have their own Dalit Christian sweeper's church once the foreigners left. Now there are many churches for "lower caste Christians" that higher caste converts simply will not attend. And neither are the sweeper converts welcomed at the churches—or the cemeteries—of upper class Christians. Old habits die hard here in the land of caste by birth.

The ingenious methods used to convert the lower castes to the Way of the Lamb are another story. Missionaries would invite unsophisticated and illiterate tribals to a big picnic, taking them along in the rear of a truck. In those early days many of them had never been in a truck and were understandably quite unfamiliar with its workings. Half way to the picnic, the driver would turn off the engine. The guests were asked to chant "Shiva, Shiva" or "Krishna, Krishna." You guessed it, Bubba, the truck wouldn't start. However when the new guests were asked to sing out "Jesus, Jesus," lo and behold the truck would fire up quite miraculously as the driver remembered to turn the key. Educated Hindus still bristle at the thought of such forms of persuasion.

Personally, I do not bewail the sweeper lady's fate for the simple reason that she doesn't either. In fact in a country where there are countless poor, she feels lucky to have a job. Any unwelcomed sympathy I could offer her would be resented as an imposition. If she ever decides to flex her union muscle and go on strike, she can hold the entire town of Damoh hostage to their own trash, though I wonder if the people who throw rubbish where they stand would even notice. Westerners who attack the caste system forget that the West has its own caste system that is as rigid and harsh as that which is seen in India. Caste is why we Californians import Mexicans to build our houses, then clean them and cart away our garbage after we have moved in. If migrant Mexican pickers in the fertile San Joachin Valley of Central California ever opted to up their caste, then vegetable prices would easily quadruple. The patina of equality that is offered to illegal workers in America is a mere inducement into more service. In truth no two people can ever be equal because each soul is unique. You who are reading these words know many things that I do not, and therefore I cannot be equal to you.

The analogous body of the social order described in the Vedic *shastras* likens the intellectual to the head; the soldier to the arms; the businessman to the belly; and the worker to the feet. If America has succeeded in some areas where India has failed, it is in the simple acknowledgement that the feet are part of the body. The labor class or "feet" are part of the body and any sane government will care for its workforce. Today India out of base miserliness has amputated its own feet, and then wonders why it can only crawl forward. In America even garbage men, or rather sanitary engineers, are paid a living wage that only boosts the economy from the bottom. Indian economy is a study in paisa wise and rupee foolish. Yet India, despite her material difficulties, still holds the unlocked treasure chest of atma jnan or spiritual knowledge, the greatest gift to the world.

Known properly as *varnashram dharma*, the caste system in its original unpolluted form was actually a very good way to organize society according to individual merits. Caste by birth as seen today is actually a perverted reflection of the original. Originally, *varnashram* was a means of social organization that was based fully upon individual merit rather than your father's occupation. In Vedic India members of lower castes could overcome social boundaries and become elevated to higher levels. There is an old story of a lad who wished to become a *brahman* disciple of a sage. The guru asked him, "What is your caste, my son?"

The boy answered, "I do not know."

"Then tell me about your father."

"Sir, my mother was a prostitute and I do not know my father's identity."

"Well, then, your father must be a *brahman* because the quality of a *brahman* is truthfulness, and you are truthful. I will accept you as my disciple."

Corrupt social leaders—or shall we call them call them "misleaders," have imposed today's rigid and seemingly irreversible system of caste-by-birth. All over the world you will find teachers (*brahmans*), soldiers (*kshatriyas*), business people (*vaishyas*), and workers (*shudras*), positions based upon quality of work and not upon birth. Arguments against Indian society's corrupt caste-by-birth system are very logical. Consider the following example. Say you are on a plane and you see the pilot drinking and socializing with the stewardesses. "Who's flying the jet?" you ask.

You are told, "Oh don't worry, the pilot's son is in the cockpit."

"Well, is he a licensed pilot?" you push on.

Then you are told, "Don't worry, Sir, he may have no training but the son of a pilot must also be a pilot."

You know that soon the plane you are on will be out of control, just as India has flown out of control due to the false imposition of the caste-by-birth system. Neither is the son of a *brahman* qualified to be a *brahman* simply on the basis of birth. Generally the blame for ruining India's social order is aimed at unfit *brahmans* who did not care to qualify themselves through study, penance and austerity. For selfish reasons unqualified men have blocked the vertical elevation of other fit souls, thereby locking others into the caste they were perceived as being born into.

True *brahmans* have qualified themselves through the cultivation of these four pillars: mercy, truthfulness, austerity and cleanliness. These analogous four legs of the bull of *dharma* have become crippled through the rampant sins of kali yuga: meat-eating, gambling, intoxication and illicit sex. In the Vedic Age great kings had no reservations about removing their crowns and kneeling before the true scion of the first order, the *brahman*.

In fact the future corruption of varnashram dharma was described in the *Varaha Purana* thousands of years ago. The *Puranas* predicted that *brahman* husbands, failing to follow proper *samskara* rituals for the procreation of good population, would impregnate their wives with souls of demons. Any farmer knows that a good crop can result only through careful cultivation. Yet this is a lesson that has bypassed many prospective parents. As a result, today you will meet so-called *brahmans* eating beef and making merry with loose women, all the while bragging about their high caste. Today too many so-called *brahmanas* are nothing more than useless descendants of a once noble line.

The fallen position of the modern *brahman* in India has been made abundantly clear to me on a thousand occasions, but two incidents stand out in my mind. Once at Calcutta's horribly crowded Sealdah Station I set upon by a gang of thieves and soon the other Bengalis milling about turned on me like vultures. This mob attack turned into a full-fledged riot and went on for nearly an hour. I was stripped naked in the streets. A last moment arrival of the police saved me being beaten to death on the street. Later at the lock-up I got to meet many of our attackers. Several of the perpetrators had rich sounding *brahman* names, like Chaturvedi ("knower of the four Vedas"), Mukhopadhyaya ("spokesperson for society") and Bhattacharya ("holy teacher").

Similarly, in Varanasi a group of *brahman* priests at the famous Vishwanath Temple attempted to waylay me. With their *brahman* threads prominently visible over their fat bellies, nearly a dozen of them blocked my way and tried to force me into a back alleyway. It is for these reasons of social corruption that great reformers like Guru Nanak sought to eliminate casteism. Srila Prabhupada took on an even greater task: the re-establishment of a once-noble society based upon quality and not birth.

While lower castes are called untouchable, some *brahmans* consider themselves untouchable due to being above reproach. The tragic fact is that unfit *brahmans* have only made recognition that much harder for the many genuine and noble *brahmans* who to this day carry the torch of *dharma* onward against all odds. That visitor to India who gets the rare association of a genuine *brahman* should consider himself blessed. India's genuine brahmans would like to see the demise of the corrupt *brahmans* more than anyone else. The baby should not be thrown out with the bath water.

Because I have not come here to change anything but myself, I have finally acquired the knack of survival in this difficult country. Unlike the moralist who seeks to superimpose upon a foreign landscape a standard suitable for another time and clime, I have no dreams about fixing India. An Indian journalist once quipped that if he were to become Prime Minister, his first act would be to commit suicide. Surely the gears were turning at their own speed before I came here and will continue spinning at their own pace after I leave. I am nothing more than an atomic spirit soul begging for mercy at the feet of my guru maharaj. I can either agree to revolve with the cycle of India's go-round, or get thrown out of the gears by enforcing my own concepts of timing upon the wheel. India will no sooner agree to change its course to appease the whim of some well-meaning altruist, than the seasonal rhythms of life can be altered at will. The monsoon will not follow autumn without winter, spring and summer in between. If there is any lesson to be imbibed from the practice of motorcycle yoga, it is that we riders are merely insignificant.

Misguided predictions found in 19th century volumes of the British missionaries still stored in the British Museum Library stating that "no Hindu would remain in India by the 21st century" have gone far astray. Indeed, 16th century Hindu predictions that the religion of India would sweep the world in the 20th century have proven more accurate. Today Hindu *swamis* have themselves set up camp all over the world. Just as many Christian missionaries were sincere apostles of their *Bible*, whereas others had exploitation pure and simple on their minds, so it is with today's Hindu preachers in Europe and America. Some *yogis* are quite sincere representatives of their culture, and others are physical embodiments of the bad *karma* created by ill-intentioned religious preachers. Undeniably a few of the suburb *yogis* have proven to be scoundrels, leaving a swath of devastated disciples in their wake. There is the well-known example of the Indian *swami* who initiated many of his men disciples into the renounced order so that he could sleep with their wives. The humble sweeper lady has inspired me into a spiral of thought, yet it has to end somewhere, and the road goes on.

Allowing the Enfield to pass the cloth bazaars, I move onward through the lanes where ladies come to buy grains from Sindhi merchants (for Lakshmi the Goddess of Fortune will not live in the house where grains are not stored). I end up at the place where items for worship or *puja* are sold, incense, ghee lamps, brass bells and the like. As in the rest of India, merchants in Damoh's bazaars cluster together. Some of the things that they sell I can't fathom, yet it will all fall into place when I find the right person to ask. Sometimes finding where to begin inquiry is the biggest challenge, for the ability to unlock even open secrets is the skill of but a few. When finding where to begin inquiry becomes the biggest challenge, I simply turn the throttle, for there will be more brain teasers around the next corner. Somehow India will always offer more questions than answers.

As I enter narrow lanes hardly six feet wide, no one gives me a second glance. Every day is laissez-faire day here in the heartland of the world's strangest country. Passing old temples that have stood where they stand now since before any roads were built, it is obvious that in their obstinate dignity they have forced the tiny by-ways to be carved around them. Skinny boys perched upon 125cc Hero-Hondas or 100cc Bajaj-Kawasakis whiz around me from all sides. Those that zoom headlong towards me with a driver and two passengers behind appear for a moment like young, three-headed motorcycle demigods coming straight for me.

I love Damoh because I love India. The whole town, unfathomable as it is, reminds me of poem I once read by Sam Walter Foss:

The Calf Path

One day through the primeval wood
A calf walked home, as a good calf should.
He made a trail all bent askew,
A crooked trail as all calves do.

Since then three hundred years have fled,
And I infer the calf is dead.
But still he left behind a trail,
And thereby hangs my moral tale.

The trail was taken up next day,
By a lone dog that passed that way.
And then a wise bellwether sheep,
Pursued the trail o'er vale and steep.

And drew the flocks behind him, too,
As good bellwethers always do.
And from that day, o'er hill and glade,
Through those woods a path was made.

And many men wound in and out,
And dodged and turned and bent about;
And uttered words of righteous wrath,
Because 'twas such a crooked path.

Yet still each followed — do not laugh,
The first migration of the path;
And through the winding woodway stalked,
Because he wobbled when he walked.

This forest path became a lane,
That bent and turned and turned again.
Then soon the lane became a road,
Where many a donkey with his load,
Toiled on beneath the burning sun,
And travelled some three miles in one.

O soon a century had past,
Each trod the footsteps of the calf.
The years passed on in swiftness fleet,

The road became a village street.
Then quite before they were aware,
Became a crowded thoroughfare.

And soon the central street was this,
Of a renowned metropolis.
Still men two centuries and a half,
Trod in the footsteps of the calf.

Each day a hundred thousand rout,
Followed the zigzag calf about;
And o'er that crooked journey went,
The traffic of a continent.

A hundred thousand men were led
By one calf near three centuries dead.
They followed still his crooked way,
And lost one hundred years a day.

For this such reverence is but
Too well established precedent.
A moral lesson this might teach,
Were I ordained and called to preach.

For men are prone to go it blind,
Along the calf paths of the mind
And work away from sun to sun
To do whate'er other men have done.

They, following the beaten path,
And out and in and forth and back,
And still their devious course pursue,
To keep the path that others do.

But how the wise wood-god would laugh,
Who saw the first primeval calf.
Ah, many things this tale would teach,
But I am not ordained to preach.

Here in Damoh, unlike Delhi, there are no ingenious plots to net the sightseer's rupee because today the entire foreign tourist industry equals me. Besides, there are ways to distinguish old-world Hindu charm from the shark-like grins of greedy hucksters who have learned of the American's weakness for bargains and casual friendships. In fact, the only souvenir that I am in search of is a tank of petrol for the Enfield to run through its Mikuni carburetor on the road out of Damoh. Strategically placed at the outskirts of town I find "The Oil Company That Cares." Since I don't want to be tricked into paying for gas that has already been sold, I first check to see that the gas pump has been reset to zero before unlocking the chrome cover on my tank. The huge wad of rupee notes that the attendant has in his front pocket is as greasy as the black rag in his back pocket. In fact there is not a square inch of his clothes or body that is not smeared with some petroleum product or another.

All around the station lie mangy semi-wild village dogs. Testifying that each one of them has made a home at this "gas station that cares" is the thick layer of telltale grease covering each as he sleeps peacefully in the morning Sun. Village dogs territorially running in packs are something you get used to seeing in India. They are not unlike our world leaders whose chorus of barking can be heard from outside the walls of the United Nations. I know that if they felt they could get away with it, this wild pack would tear off my limbs in a Damoh second, which equals about one quarter New York hour. Perhaps the uneasy peace I have established with the dogs is based upon their fear of me because I vote.

Recently in a nearby village a jackal came out of the woods and attacked a farmer. The stray dogs that the farmer had been feeding summarily proceeded to rip the jackal to shreds. When the farmer came down with rabies and died a few days later, sadly all the dogs of this particular pack were hunted down and killed.

India somehow gives a new meaning to "a dog's life." At train stations, three-legged dogs are common; careless animals whose tongue made them stay upon the track when their ears were telling them to go. I have even seen one-legged dogs groveling for food. Here in a land where life's grimmest aspects are subject to the viewing of any idle witness, I once observed a dog getting his tail amputated by a train's wheel. When I told one fellow American wayfarer of the incident, he related casually how he had seen a train roll over a man's neck leaving a headless torso lying innocuously at some nameless Indian railway depot. Apparently it is a common form of suicide in a land where those who commit suicide are said to return as ghosts, bound to the subtle body, and condemned to re-enact their final deed for a very long time. Hindus consider suicide as a way out for cowards who cannot tolerate their own karma, who do not have the faith to right their own wrongs. But then the one-legged dog forces us to ponder like some Zen monk, what is the sound of one paw clapping? Neither does the headless torso laugh. The attendant takes my rupees casually.

Damoh is everything I had expected to see, and less. London, Paris, Rome, Damoh, it will not likely be written up in any future tourist guidebook. It is still morning now and the roads through green fields beckon. At the town's edge the morning Sun showers his rays upon a troupe of ladies sitting in a circle by a green field, singing happily while taking a break from planting.

Out here, wheeling just yards away from the Indo-urban mini-turmoil that is Damoh, it becomes easy to see why all ancient civilizations worshipped the Sun god. In Sanskrit the Sun is called Mitra, or friend. He is not some impersonal ball of light, but a well wisher, the king of daytime, and the Universal life-giver. He is also the great hour hand on the Universal Clock that each of us must sooner or later acknowledge, as daily that clock ticks away the irretrievable moments that comprise a mortal's life. The Sun god may be worshipped for the warmth he provides, or disparaged when his rays become unbearable. But he can never be criticized for abandoning his bright nature, even as rain clouds gather beneath him. He is just like Krishna who smiled in transcendence as He drove Arjuna's chariot into the raging storm of the Battle of Kurukshetra. He who can level the charge that the Sun has ever been unfaithful to his nature is yet to be born. Rather, since the beginning of timeless time, man has been obliged to set his pattern of life by the movements of the Sun.

And before Mitra, my friend the Sun, crosses his noon apex in his horse-drawn chariot, becoming harsh and angry in the afternoon sky, I must make time on the savage road out of Damoh.

At Parashurama Kunda

CHAPTER FIVE

The Devi Road
"The Eightfold Path on Highway Seven"

TEMPLES OF THE MOTHER GODDESS DURGA DEVI are found in every part of India. The goddess is worshipped upon hilltops and on riverbanks; deep within wild forests and in crowded bazaars that have grown up around her shrines. She is Vindhyavasini, goddess of the Vindhya Hills; Trinayani, the "three-eyed"; Banjari, The forest-dweller; Kanya Kumari, virgin goddess (of the three oceans). One reason why there are so many temples to her is explained in the *Puranas*. Once upon a time while Lord Shiva meditated in his Himalayan abode, his wife Sati, who is none other than the goddess herself, observed that the *devatas* were flying overhead. The demigods were on their way to celebrate a gala festival—a *yagna*—below in the foothills alongside the roaring Ganges. Now the sponsor of this grand religious affair was Sati's father Daksha. Sati pleaded with her husband Shiva, master of the *yogis*, "My Lord, it is natural even for a young bride to miss her family. Please do me the honor by escorting me to my father's gala festival."

With a gentle smile Lord Shiva admonished, "O Devi, we are happy here in the company of each other at our mountaintop hermitage, engaged in the bliss of *yoga* and self-realization. This *yagna* of your father Daksha is being attended by materialists whose association is best avoided. Please do not go but stay by my side in the bliss of spiritual trance."

Sati's father was narrow-minded and could not appreciate the greatness of Lord Shiva. Although Sati knew that her husband would never consider attending a function where he would be disrespected, she decided to go anyway, for family attachment is quite difficult to transcend.

When Sati arrived at the sacrificial site in Kankhal, her father Daksha met her with his sharp criticism of her husband. Sati could not brook any insult spoken against her husband, greatest of the *yogis,* so she expertly countered each of Daksha's deluded remarks with clear arguments of her own. Then in a fit of rage she declared, "O father, this useless body has emanated from you, therefore it is contaminated and impure. I cannot live as the daughter of one who is blind to Lord Shiva's unfathomable glories." With that, in the presence of Daksha and all the gods and sages assembled there, Sati assumed a posture of *yogic* meditation. Moments later an all-consuming fire sprang from her extremities. As her body was reduced to ashes in an instant, Sati's spiritual essence, her *atma,* flew off to be reborn as Parvati, daughter of the god of the mountains, Himavat.

Through his mystic vision, Shiva, who is known as Trinayana or "three-eyed," witnessed all that had taken place. He called for his bull carrier Nandi. Soon he appeared at the site of the *yagna* accompanied by a terrible entourage of ghouls and goblins, laughing hysterically like one gone mad. As Lord Shiva's dark associates set about destroying the *yagna-shala,* Shiva tenderly picked up the charred remains of his beloved Sati.

At that time, the Supreme Lord Vishnu, the enjoyer of all acts of sacrifice, appeared and asked Shiva from many angles of *yoga* philosophy, why he was lamenting for a dead body from which the spirit had departed. To underscore his point, Lord Vishnu sent down his razor sharp *chakra* cutting Sati's lifeless body into many pieces. These body parts fell at various places throughout the Indian sub-continent and became the fifty-one *shakti-pithas,* or "places sacred to the goddess of prowess and energy." Eventually temples of *devi* worship would arise at each one.

The Devi Road, National Highway Seven, passes through the majextic rocky peaks of the Vindhyachal

The hair of the goddess fell at Mathura, the topmost *shakti-pith*, where she is called Chamunda. At Naimisharanya, the center of the Universe, fell Sati's heart and there she is adored as Lalita. In Guwahati her private area fell to earth. The river turns red there for three days each year, and she is worshipped in a great temple as Kamakshi, "fulfiller of desires." Four toes of her left foot fell to Earth at Calcutta where she is revered as Kali, the "black" Goddess. Her earrings landed at Manikarnika Ghat beside the Ganges at Varanasi, the beginning point of the Devi Road. The *devi's* tongue became the shooting flame of fire called Jwalamukhi, which springs from the snow-bound slopes of Himachal. The goddess' elbow is worshipped at Ujjain as Harsiddhi, protector and benefactress of godly emperors, like the immortal King Vikramaditya from whose reign the Indian year is measured. At Puri fell the goddess' navel where her devotees revere her as Vimala, "the spotless." On a hill above Rajastan's Pushkar Lake fell to earth the *devi's* wrists, where Her devotees adore her as Gayatri, "deliverer from sin." The fingers of both hands of the goddess fell at Prayaga, one of the five great holy places, near the spot where three holy rivers meet called *triveni-sangam*.

Some of these fifty-one *shakti-pithas* are very well known like the temple at Kali Ghat, visited by millions each year. Others have been neglected, while still others have been altogether forgotten, awaiting future re-discovery. Many of them are in Pakistan and Bangladesh, lost to the partition of India. Still others are claimed at two or more sites.

The temple of Sharada Devi two hundred miles north of Jabalpur at Maihar is said to be one of the fifty-one *shakti-piths,* where Sati's necklace fell to earth. Whatever the history of this particular site, it is sure and certain that Goddess Sharada's popularity has grown in recent years, and her magnetic pull can be felt in all parts of middle India. Certainly, the heart of the heartland belongs to Sharada Devi.

When I observed the portrait or deity of Goddess Sharada in hundreds of homes, shops and temples I visited around the Jabalpur district, I developed a desire to pilgrimage to her hilltop abode. One day in early *vasant*, the spring season, and on a day that the stars shone favorably, I cranked up the Enfield, destination Maihar. By the Hindu system of *jyotish* or astrology, I was born under the earthy feminine sign of Kanya *rashi*, Moon in Virgo, which is said to be the same sign that governs India. Ruled by Mercury, we travel-loving Virgos tend not to take the direct road to any destination, whether physical or mental. Instead our choice will be an out-of-the way route that provides fertile ground for thought and discovery. So I have charted the Virgo's way, a short two-day's trip visiting other temples and friends along the way.

Sun rays shoot from behind the Vindhyachal peaks as I turn north onto the road to Devi. On my right a crow, stolen berry within his beak, swallows and caws twice. A young housewife holding a full pot of yogurt between her two fine hands, cautiously checks the traffic from every direction, then darts right in front of me. These omens tell me that the trip will be a successful one as the early morning smells of cooking, of *puja* and of a world greeting a new day invigorate the ride.

Not ten miles beyond the Chungi Choki crossroads, I am forced to slow way down to a crawl. Road work ahead, a stretch of National Highway Seven is being paved for the hundredth time by tribal men and women. Workers queue up in a semi-circular line, scoop up rocks that have earlier been dumped there, and carry the pebbles on their heads to the newly-grated roadway, hurling down their load with an effective twirling motion. Each worker is paid a wage of about Rs.45 daily. Mothers set their babies on the rock pile while they work, until the little ones grow hungry and need to nurse. Doubtless each of these road builders likewise slept upon gravel in their own infancy. It is upon the shoulders of these *adi-vasis*, the so-called "backward class," that rests the responsibility of knitting a sub-continent together with a maze of asphalt. How these workers arrive at work is another story.

In the morning a huge tractor made by either HMT (Hindustan Machine Tools) or Eicher (which now owns Enfield India) ambles through fields and dirt tracks into the jungle to fetch several generations of able-bodied men and women, all willing workers. About thirty can load into the trailer behind the tractor, provided they all stand, and in this way they are brought to the site. By the same means the *adi-vasis* are returned to the jungle in the evening. It is this plodding never-ending method of road construction that accounts for the vastly varied conditions upon a single stretch of highway. Few of these dark-skinned tribals own even bicycles, hence their hand crafted highways are meant for an India that is entirely different than the one they know.

The din and chaos of the roadwork test the limits of my patience in the hot Sun, but then India is nothing but a series of tests. Whosoever enjoys India is the type of person who enjoys being tested. With a few daredevil moves that the average scootering schoolgirl would consider ordinary, I slalom through the dusty roadwork in less than half an hour, and soon the wind caused by the speed of the bike is drying my cotton garments. After an hour I turn east onto the dirt countryside track to Majholi, a village that lies ten miles off the Devi Road. A pair of red foxes standing sociably by the roadside spots me and, turning quickly, disappears into the tall grasses. In a tree above me female black-faced Hanuman monkeys care for a young member by turns. Soon I enter the village.

Majholi has grown around an extremely rare temple of Vishnu Varaha, the "boar incarnation of Godhead." Sometimes the Lord is impelled to take the form of one of the species of His own creations. Once He became a turtle named Kurma, and on another occasion He became a fish named Matsya. How He decided to descend in His boar *avatar*, as Lord Vishnu Varaha, is narrated in many of the *Puranas*.

Many, many years ago, due to the exploitation of the Earth by the demon Hiranyaksha, the world fell into the nether regions at the bottom of the Universe. Only Shri Vishnu, "the all-pervasive," was capable of uplifting the Earth globe from the accumulated muck. Yet how could the Lord of the Universe, who is called Jagadish, be expected to retrieve the planet from such an impure place? The solution was found when Lord Vishnu Himself manifested His form as Varaha, the boar incarnation. After slaying the demon Hiranyaksha, the "golden-eyed," in a pitched battle lasting many years, the Lord Boar went all the way down to Patala-loka and lifted up the Earth by supporting it upon His twin tusks.

Like many of the temple deities of Central India, the huge stone *murti* worshipped in Majholi is said to be self-manifested. Locals tell the story of a mysterious wild pig that used to run through the fields here, hundreds of years ago. The farmers were worried as the rampaging boar was ruining their crops. Not long after that a fisherman found a small stone Deity in the form of a boar in a nearby lake, which he took home. However, this peculiar Deity soon began to grow by His own will. Eventually Lord Vishnu Varaha reached His present immovable size of several tons in weight. Locals hailed the miracle by building a temple around Him. As the village of Majholi grew up around the temple, a place of pilgrimage was born.

Through unpaved dusty lanes the bike carries me to the temple of Lord Vishnu Varaha. Fortune is with me and I have arrived at the time of the ringing of the *aratik* bells and clanging of gongs that call all nearby devotees to the noontime service. I rush inside and listen meditatively as village ladies sing *bhajans* while the white robed *pandit* conducts the service. I try not to be surprised that the Deity, which would appear as a mere stone statue to the uninitiated, emanates a feeling of joy and victory which surrounds all present. Although in the form of a boar, He is worshiped here as none other than the Supreme Personality of Godhead, the ocean of bliss, and shelter of His devotees.

When the ceremony ends, I become pleasantly surprised that Panditji, the *pujari* or priest, remembers me from an earlier visit. I am honored by the offer of lunch with his family. At his modest house nearby, we sit upon the cement floor, eating the standard fare of *dal-subji-roti*—soup, vegetables and *chapattis*

The ever-blissful Lord of the Universe assumed the form of a boar, Lord Vishnu Varaha, just to lift the world from the nether regions.

—on *patals* or disposable plates made of leaves. As I take my last bite, fully satisfied, I notice that *panditji,* a perfect gentleman, has timed the finishing of his meal with me. It is through little details like this that the Hindu host honors his culture, one that dictates *atithi devo bhava*: "the guest is God." After dinner his youngest daughter pours water over my hands on instruction from her mother, and I do the customary mouth rinsing. What infinite kindness and patience these devotees of the Vedic culture possess.

It is the afternoon now and each villager will rest for an hour or two. I must make my way back to the Devi Road so I turn down Panditji's invitation to rest upon the porch. I steer into the direction of the town of Sihora, which has been built around an extinct volcano, and upon this volcano is a temple to the goddess Jwalamukhi, the "fire-tongued." As the temple has closed for the afternoon so that the deity can rest, I simply bow my head in the direction of the *mandir* as I slowly roll by.

A few miles north of Sihora I rejoin National Highway Seven, my Devi Road, and just ahead an excited procession catches my eye. There beside the road is a man rolling over and over slowly heading northbound, smiling beatifically in the dust. Beside him a middle-aged woman is wheeling a cart upon which an altar of pictures to the goddess, incense and flowers have been placed. Upon the altar cart sits an old lady, likely his mother. Suddenly I remember an article that a few weeks earlier I had chanced to notice in the *Jabalpur Chronicle*.

The austere roling pilgrim of Maihar.

This rolling man is from Indore some three hundred miles to the southwest. He had taken a vow, for what reason I do not know, to roll along the roadway the entire distance from Indore to the doorstep of Goddess Sharada at Maihar. Some six or seven months of rolling down this highway are behind him, yet this pilgrim has before him at least two months until he reaches the lotus feet of the Mother of the Universe. His interpretation of rolling down the road to the door of the *devi* is different than mine because my rolling two wheels have but two hours or so before they reach Maihar. But then in the world of *yoga* there is also room for individual interpretation because each soul is unique. Each entity is singular in the quest for liberation, and achieving transcendence is likewise an individual endeavor since personality remains in the state of the soul liberated from matter.

I put the Enfield on its side stand and walk over to the procession buzzing about the rolling man. He has achieved some kind of celebrity status. I cannot hide my curiosity mixed with admiration for his crazy austerity. As I make a small offering to his altar to help his entourage with their daily expenses, I am surprised that he looks up to smile at me blissfully, a smile that says that he is doing exactly what he has chosen to do. Sometimes in the vast, great, austere and strange world that is India all you can do is step back with wonder. Certainly this man and the people walking with him are doing something only few men have ever done. Yet would the goddess have been any less pleased if, say, he had gone by bus or had just hopped upon a motorcycle? The answer does not lie with me.

Half an hour beyond the rolling man I find my faithful wheels rolling through Sleemanabad, a town with a very unusual history. Known as Kohka until the mid-1800's, Sleemanabad is one of the few places in today's India named for a European. Col. William Sleeman was a British officer stationed in Jabalpur in the 1830's. At that time there was a gang of murderous dacoits, called *thuggees*, active in Jabalpur District. In fact unchallenged *thuggee* gangs had been waylaying unsuspecting wayfarers for several centuries. They were past masters of deception; they would cook and entertain pilgrims, yet when the leader called "bring the tobacco" the end was near. Each dacoit would then whip out a yellow scarf weighted with a silver coin and slowly strangle his victim to death. These *thuggees*, or *pindaris* as they called themselves, surrounded their blood-thirst for death with a concocted form of goddess worship. The *thuggees* were, of course, no more devoted to the goddess–the Mother of all life–than American Satanists who perform ritual orgies and blood sacrifices before a cross are to Christ.

The *thuggees* were an entrenched problem, one that travelers truly feared, when Col. William H. Sleeman was appointed District Collector on behalf of

Her Majesty's government. The colonel took strong measures to root out this *pindari* cult of freebooting highwaymen to the extent of even having his own spies infiltrate their inner circle. The novel by Calcutta-born John Masters, and later Ivory-Merchant movie, *The Deceivers*, was loosely based upon the life of Col. Sleeman of Jabalpur. In that movie Pierce Brosnan plays Sleeman. In his day Col. Sleeman was hailed as a genuine hero not only by the British, but by the Hindus as well, for the strong measures he was forced to take to subdue the barbaric cult. Over 3600 *thugees*, many of whom had murdered hundreds, were arrested through his efforts, and of these nearly 500 were executed. Locals say that the tree where many were hanged still grows in Jabalpur. But Sleeman saved the most brutal form of punishment for the most vicious of the gang. He had their skulls crushed like an eggshell under the foot of an elephant while the public looked on in satisfaction and in horror. Col. Sleeman wrote several books on the *thuggees* and spoke seven languages including the *thuggees'* secret Ramasi dialect.

Ancient Hindu lore which tells of the appearance of Goddess Kali, whom the *thuggees* claimed to worship, actually offers proof that she cannot be supplicated by scoundrels like the *thuggees*. Rather, Goddess Kali is the enemy of evil as seen by the narration of her history from the *Markendeya Purana*. Once there was a demon named Raktabija, or "blood-seed," who received the boon that should any drop of his blood touch the ground, then that drop would arise as a duplicate of himself. In this way Raktabija, feeling that he had become invincible, set about waging war against the demigods. As the arrows and

Thumbs up, Dude...and welcome to the jungle. These black-faced Hannuman monkeys, highly intelligent, are respected as descendants of Lord Rama's army. Many will descend from their trees to eat from our hand.

spears hurled by the gods against Raktabija pierced his body, drops of his blood only served to create a new army of Raktabija duplicates, each as fierce as the original. Goddess Kali, "the black," then appeared as an expansion of Goddess Durga, who in turn is an expansion of Shiva's wife Parvati. In order to stop the attacks of Raktabija, she was forced to drink his blood before it hit the ground. In this way the black goddess wiped out the army of thousands of duplicate Raktabijas, furious at his audacity in challenging the *devatas*.

Yet still her rampage continued. In order to pacify the anger of this incarnation of the Mother of the Universe, Lord Shiva lay down before her. As quite by accident she placed her foot upon the chest of Mahadeva, her tongue protruded from her mouth in horror and atonement for her deed. Raktabija had been defeated, and now Kali too became pacified. Peace again reigned in *swarga*, home of the demigods.

From the history of the appearance of Mother Kali, we can understand that the black goddess has no interest in the death of innocent people. Neither is she interested in the offerings of goats that are "sacrificed" at some of her temples, for Kali Maa herself is a vegetarian. It would be a grave injustice therefore to hold the Hindu world responsible for the concocted and fanciful exploits of a gang of thugs, even those who try to disguise their brutality behind a veil of religion. Local legend states that Col. Sleeman actually made offerings at a temple of the goddess near present-day Sleemanabad, after which his French Mauritian wife was blessed with a son, whom the couple named Arthur. It was after the birth of Arthur on the sixth of January 1833; that he gave land for the upkeep of the temple, and the town of Kokha was renamed Sleemanabad. It is said that descendants of Col. Sleeman have visited Sleemanabad and likewise have been blessed with sons. Today, in the temple of the goddess here in Sleemanabad, an "eternal flame" is kept lit in the colonel's honor.

Today Sleemanabad for all its history is no different from any other Central Indian village. Still I promise myself I will explore the place on my return journey. Right now I have an appointment with the Devi Road and with Goddess Sharada, the Mother of the Universe. And the Sun is moving towards the western sky.

A crowd of laughing village school children attracts my attention near the highway. Curious, I am hardly noticed as I make my way into their circle. The forced antics of a performing monkey chained to his trainer have captured their attention. The irony is that although monkeys are seen throughout India, even in cities, people will still pay money to laugh at the performance of one pathetically chained. In fact, the Hindu scriptures consider monkeys to be a "sub-human" species that falls between man and the quadrupeds. I once witnessed an

Within the Jabalpur jungle is this shrine to Lord Parashurama, which has not been seen by other foreigner's eyes in living memory. Woodsman Krishan Lal Guards the area, axe in hand.

itinerant *yogi* trying to explain to one such monkey trainer, "Not only is this monkey chained to you, but by the laws of *karma* you are chained to the monkey since he provides your livelihood. You will be a monkey and he will be a man in your next lives. At that time you will repay him when you are chained and forced to dance for him." An English friend of mine once bought a monkey from such a trainer just to let him go. In fact the crowd loved that act the best.

The afternoon ride from Sleemanabad to Maihar, though fatiguing and hot, is peaceful–even blissful–and blessedly uneventful. Indeed, it is a handlebar trance of about three hours weaving, speeding, slowing, downshifting, speeding and second-guessing all others on the road before me. All the while the great chant for deliverance, the Hare Krishna *mantra*, is keeping time in my mind with the purposeful beat of the piston.

Now in the afternoon I am riding with my Indian helmet on as a shield from the Sun. By the standards of Western riding gear, at about three dollars, this helmet is practically useless for protection from anything except sunstroke. Out of the thousands of two-wheeled riders that I will see on the road today, only one or two others will be wearing a helmet. In Delhi where protective headgear has recently been mandated by law, riders wear anything that resembles a helmet. There, plastic-domed men on scooters all look like amateur construction foremen. Many tie their "helmets" on with a shoestring.

As I approach the outskirts of my destination of Maihar, I slow the Enfield down to the effortless crawl of a country bicycle, the sometimes tedious pace at which this giant country moves, to take it all in. I have made good time and I am in no hurry. Tonight I shall behold the evening *aratik*. From the roadside I am accosted by a *yogi* whose body appears as coarse and black as a water buffalo's. I've spoken of my weakness for visiting holy places and temples, and I am likewise seized by curiosity whenever I meet sages of any and all schools. Although I take an instant disliking to this *yogi,* I keep my feelings hidden, remaining outwardly respectful. India's vast majority of *yogis* are genuine, while the remainder could be classed as posers to varying degrees. Yet here as elsewhere it is always the antics of the few buffoons that sully the good name of sincere ascetics.

There is a genuine flaw in us mortals who are wont to reason: "I have survived thus far, therefore I shall survive in the future." We ignore that mishap and disasters happen all about, and continue believing that we shall live forever in the fool's paradise with which we have cloaked ourselves. We stand smug and proud behind our phalanx of fallible soldiers. It is with a fatal fascination veiled by self-assurance that I park the bike and strut over to meet the black *yogi*, greeting him with folded hands. He grins back, probably a bit too much, and invites me into his straw hut. I notice that I am being escorted a bit aggressively. Once inside, I am horrified: all around the walls hang grinning human skulls. My God! I have entered the secret world of a *tantric*. It is not merely a cliché that curiosity killed the cat.

Foolishly, I accept the invitation to sit before him, feigning invulnerability like one who believes his time on earth has not yet been spent. At least I can choose one of two reasons for not bolting, fear or stupidity; and looking back I was probably too stupid to be afraid at this point. He motions to a burlap bag before him, and I sit down upon it cross-legged. To allay any misgivings, the black *yogi* begins with a little casual conversation in English, which few genuine *yogis* know or care to speak. He says that he is a Tamil from Malaysia, boasting that he is a close relative of Swami Shivananda of Rishikesh. This especially fails to impress me since I was treated inhospitably by the disciples when I visited his *ashram* in the Himalayan foothills some years earlier.

Deftly, the black *yogi* whips out a filthy pipe–a *chillam*–and indicates that I too should smoke *ganja*, Indian marijuana, with him. He is surprised when I politely refuse, since any white man who may have strayed into his clutches was probably a hippie. Undaunted, he puffs away lustily. Soon the tiny hut is filled with a dark cloud of thick smoke. He has forced me to unwittingly breathe intoxicating fumes. Escaping the doping effect becomes impossible. Observing that I am gradually being overcome, the black *yogi* puts the pipe aside and begins to sing like a smitten opera tenor. He chants, casually at first, then rapidly, "I love you, I love you, I l-o-o-o-o-ve you." Now disarmed, I muse to myself that I have never met such a crooning buffoon and wonder if he is just some harmless fraud. But he is a clown with a very dark sense of humor. Still, I have not yet realized the danger in which I have I placed myself.

Suddenly, the black *yogi* changes his mood and begins chanting intensely one of the Sanskrit *bija* or "seed" *mantras*. No longer singing in the clouds, he has now knitted his brows and is focusing his black, angry and evil eyes right upon me with the precision of a laser beam. *"Ang, ang, ang, a-n-n-n-n-g"* he vibrates hypnotically as suddenly I drop into a deep and induced sleep, eyes rolling and chin upon my chest. I am now overpowered by the force of the mystic's sound vibration and am helplessly afloat like one drugged. Suddenly a tiny voice arises from somewhere inside me, screaming with my last bit of consciousness, *"Get up now, you fool! Can't you see that this evil yogi would like to hang the skull of a white man as a perverse trophy upon his wall?"*

Somehow I manage to abruptly jump to my feet and struggle to find the words thanking him for his "hospitality." In India genteel manners are all-important, even if someone is trying to rip you off, or even kill you. Obviously crestfallen and disappointed at the failure of his black magic and hypnotic power, the wretched *tantric* adopts a suave, devil-may-care attitude and insists that I return again after my *darshan* of the Mother Goddess. Such evil *yogis*, though a tiny minority among India's many spiritual stalwarts, are not unlike the *thuggees*. These *tantrics* lure unsuspecting and innocent victims, often young girls or children, to solitary places. There the intended sacrificial victim is offered "sacred food or *prasad* of the goddess," which usually turns out to be *dhatura* poison, as lethal as arsenic. Or the victim is tied up and ritualistically beheaded.

Some of these *yogis* actually seem to have developed minor mystic powers, and as a result enjoy a free reign because villagers fear them. The *Bhagavat Purana* narrates the story of the great devotee Jad Bharat of Kalinjar who was kidnapped by *tantrics*. When the *tantrics* tried to sacrifice Jad Bharat before the deity of Kali, the angry goddess burst forth from her temple deity form. With Her four arms she seized the knives that they were about to use in their human sacrifice, and slew each thug with his own weapon.

True *yogis* have a simple and clean appearance cultivated through temperance, sense control and austerity. They do not take intoxicants or eat meat, do not associate freely with loose women. Elevated *sadhus*, who follow the rules of *sadhana* or *yoga*, are known for their humility. They follow the old adage "the tree loaded with ripe fruit and the cloud heavy with rain both hang low." They are always respectful to women and girls bowing before them and calling them "Mother." They are very careful to follow each of the injunctions of the religious *shastras*, like daily prayerful recitations of the holy names of God. At religious *melas* the imitators are easily spotted like crows among swans because they do not observe any of the prescribed restrictions, nor do they practice the gentle tolerance of the followers of the eight-fold path of *ashtanga yoga*.

The black *yogi* accompanies me outside. I now find him truly despicable, the opposite of everything that has ever attracted me to India. Yet I hide my disgust and still remain polite. Somehow I have survived by just barely outsmarting him. With a vile snort that nurses his anger, he withdraws cursing and defeated like the setting Sun covered by storm clouds. I fire the bike to freedom and reflect that without the salvation of my Enfield I could have fallen into the clutches of the black *yogi* forever.

In this strange and wonderful land I have lived with *yogis* in Himalayan caves, in desert huts, and in forest shrines. They have cared for me and nourished me and by so doing they have respected my own *guru maharaj*. I have been fed by their hands, instructed by them and have the deepest regard for the genuine ones. The black *yogi* of Maihar is an aberration upon the spiritual path. Rascals like him are an affront to all that is decent in India and the world. True *yogis* must not be judged by the sins of the predators. Perhaps this is the same plea echoed in all religions.

India is a land of extremes in every way, and the heart of India can be attained after only great endeavor. When I first came here, I thought of India as a poor country. Today I consider India to be a very rich country that is burdened with many poor. The first-time Western visitor, familiar with a television-dominated society in which virtually everyone, including the pampered household pet, belongs to varying degrees of the middle classes, becomes astounded by the extremes he witnesses everyday. We gape with pity mixed with a sense of superiority at India's poor, yet cannot fathom the vast wealth and authority owned by others at the opposite end of the spectrum. We throw a rupee or two to the diseased beggar, yet may miss the opportunity to sit before the 100-year old *yogi* whose spiritual qualities are fully awakened and whose mind is as clear as a bell. We hear of sins that are performed in the name of worship, yet refuse to acknowledge the piety and sacrifice of India's devoted masses. We have suffered the legendary rudeness of India's government officials or dishonesty of a Delhi travel agent, yet may never cross through the doorway of an Indian home to sample the hospitality there. More than any place on earth, India is a land of extremes. More often than not it will be the extremes in ugliness, disease, poverty, filth and moral degradation that we notice, giving scant credit for whatever goodness abounds; for India's virtues often remain hidden. This is not the first time visitor's fault, for this land is a difficult and daunting experience. Although India can only be approached with an open mind, still one's guard must not be let down. He who masters this simple two-pronged technique alone can succeed here. But it may take many years to master.

Just as India throws up a wall through which only determined souls may peer, so the ways of the Mother Goddess are formidable to see. Shri Ranamukhadevaji, who used to teach me Indian astrology, once commented that according to my horoscope I would always be very devoted to the *devi*. This has turned out to be true. The goddess, or female energy personified, who predominates this material world has many beautiful forms. In her eight-armed form she is called Durga, which means "citadel," because her material energies delude the mind and are as insurmountable as an impregnable fort. She is called Maya, the goddess of illusion, because he who has not been bewildered by her external energies and the false promise of fleeting pleasures is the rarest of souls. Her materialistic worshippers make plans to stay here in this world searching for the reflection of unrealized enjoyment forever. She is also Shakti, the "power, prowess and energy" behind all that happens here in this material world. Here in this world, this *devi-dham* or "citadel of the goddess," she is supreme. All men are drawn like moths to flame to her magnetism, as seen in the fleeting, sidelong glances of beautiful ladies. The lithe and youthful body we so adore is little more than a hazardous chemical dump stretched over with skin. Yet due to the goddess' power of *maya,* or material attraction, we deluded souls try to enjoy our five senses—sight, touch, smell, taste and hearing—unlimitedly.

When Lord Vishnu expands Himself into Lord Shiva, His spouse Goddess Lakshmi expands into Parvati. Parvati's husband, Lord Shiva, is an ascetic, busy with his meditation. Shiva lets his wife, or rather her expansion, Durga, control this Universe just as a householder is content to let his spouse run the daily affairs. Durga or Sharada, the Mother of the Universe, is active in all aspects of life on this material plane. Narrow-minded empiricists contradict this view of a personal Godhead supervising demigods by asserting their view that creation happened of its own accord. Though the speculators' reasoning is unfounded, they claim that planets and life forms emerged from a "primordial soup" after some cosmic "big bang."

Equally deluded are the dogmatic religionists who, though they recognize the supremacy of a one God controller, argue that He cannot have a chain of command under Him. Like these religionists, the way of the true *yogi* is monotheistic. Yet even in oneness there is differentiation, and this is the point of diversion. The philosophy of *yoga* argues that if even factory owners have managers and supervisors beneath them, then why can't God have deputized demigods.

In this world Lord Shiva is the agent of Lord Vishnu, whose all-encompassing energy pervades each atom. It is Lord Shiva's union with Parvati, the predominating deity of the female principle that injects each of thousands of billions of souls into the beginning of their life cycles over and over again. The repeated placing of each soul life after life into appropriate bodies and circumstances, is the work of other demigods. These demigods oversee the affairs of the world, and worship Shiva and Parvati as the greatest amongst them. Lord Indra controls the weather, Lord Vayu causes the wind to blow, Varuna is the god of waters, Saraswati is the goddess of learning, Agni rules fire and Yama is the controller of death.

It is the thankless task of the goddess called Durga or Sharada to test each soul by controlling the energy that deludes us birth after birth. He who awakens the dawning of *yoga* alone achieves the transcendence that propels the *jiva* soul back into his original position in spirit. When transcendental realization culminates in selfless devotion to Vishnu or Yogeshwar, the Lord of all *yogis,* then the level of *bhakti-yoga* has been realized. The ascent to the exalted platform of love of Krishna, or devotional service, is the final key to liberation from matter. He alone whose love for God is unalloyed gains freedom from Maya's prison. This is the final lesson of *yoga.*

Eventually this Universe must face destruction, too, for as it has been rightly sung, "all things must pass." Then, when the rays of Surya, the Sun demigod increase twelve-fold, Lord Shiva rises from his meditation and dances the *tandava-nritya,* "the dance of destruction." Universal destruction, or *pralaya,* when the fate of the world is sealed equals the inhalation cycle of one breath of Vishnu. That which has been born has an inevitable date with dissolution at last, and even this great Universe which maintains us has a predestined meeting with fate. At this time all the temporary demigods, like outgoing US Presidents, find that their terms of office have come to a close.

Ultimately cosmic devastation yields to creation once again as Lord Vishnu exhales. In other words, the life of this Universe equals one breath of Lord Vishnu, the blissful Chief of the gods. With Vishnu's outgoing breath, *jiva* souls that have yet to be liberated are injected through the energies of Parvati and Shiva into the newly formed Universe, as once again the cosmic wheel makes its next go-round. Lord Vishnu appoints demigods anew to control the affairs of the next Universe, as souls continue to struggle with the modes of Nature for many lifetimes and Universal cycles on their way to liberation.

Within this material world Shiva, who is Vishnu in contact with material Nature, is the supreme male; and Goddess Parvati, who is expanded from Shri Vishnu's spouse Lakshmi, is the supreme female. As explained, the balanced interaction of the energies of Shiva and Shakti, the push and pull, the embrace of the ebb and flow, that insures that this Universe will continue until its time of destiny draws nigh. The elements of this Universe—namely earth, water, fire, air, mind, intelligence and false ego—merge back with the body of Lord Vishnu with each inhalation. When He exhales, they are used once again in the construction cycle when uncountable bubble-like Universes emanate from His body and float upon the Garbhodak Ocean. The billions of years that each of these floating Universes lasts, a period of time that we of earthly vision miscalculate as infinity, is but a single divine breath of Vishnu. When Vishnu inhales, the cycle of destruction is inaugurated once again. Indeed the microcosm with its interaction of male and female energies does reflect the macrocosm.

Lord Vishnu in all His majesty is an expansion of the Supreme Personality of Godhead Shri Krishna, who lives eternally in the anti-material abode called Goloka Vrindavan. Wherever and whenever the Supreme Lord Krishna appears in His many inconceivable forms, His beloved consort Shri Radha follows Him. She becomes Vishnu's wife Lakshmi; indeed Shri Radha Herself is the ultimate origin of each of the worshipful forms of Devi. Just as this temporary world is a reflection of the eternal spiritual domain, so the *devi*, who rules this world, is the Chhaya or shadow of Radha, the original Goddess. Sometimes Radha and Krishna deign to visit this world in Their original forms. When the Divine Couple comes into view for our benefit, then together They share Their eternal pastimes here on Earth to the delight of Their devotees who only wish to serve Them eternally. Radha sports in the fields of Vraja as a young *gopi*, a cowherd girl, and consequently it becomes very difficult to understand that She alone is the source of all *shaktis*. Bewildered materialists who worship the many forms of Devi for sense gratification and riches generally have no clue as to Her spiritual origin. In the eternal abode of Vrindavana the Vrajavasis understand the secrets of Radha. Convinced that none can approach Krishna without Her mercy, they take shelter of Her Name. She is called Hara, and is the Hare of Hare Krishna, and She is the sustenance of this motorcycle *yogi*.

It is therefore with this multi-tiered frame of mind that I am on this rolling pilgrimage, riding upon the rocky road to Devi. I shall not approach the goddess to ask for wealth, fame or enjoyment. These are but entanglements that bring only the promise of future delusion in this *mrityu-loka*, the world of birth and death. I shall only see the Mother of this Universe as the very shadow of She who rules the Spiritual Sky. My prayer will be that I am joined to Her lotus feet–and ultimately to Krishna–through loving devotional service to the Divine Pair life after life, in this world or in the next.

Now, before me, I see the hill upon which lives the goddess, and my Devi Road has found its destination. By her grace I have arrived here at last, for she alone has insured my safety. Tomorrow when the time comes for my return I have faith that she will carry me just as safely home. It is a long walk up the steps to her *darshan*.

After temple adoration of Goddess Sharada, the Mother of this world, and with the pleasant sound of *aratik* bells still ringing in my head, I descend the one thousand steps down to the bike. Quite out of nowhere an austere-looking young member of the working class steps before me, and demands: "What do you want?" As my eyes meet his, I recognize an old scenario: he is just practicing a few words of English on a foreigner. These are quite possibly the only precious words that he knows of my language. He looks quite uncomprehending and even downright comical as I reply words he doubtless can not understand: "Ask the goddess. I have told her everything."

The vast, majestic and mutable land of India is protected on three sides by the waters of three oceans. Her great expanse is made fertile by the ceaseless flow of many rivers running in every direction. The great Godavari rushing from the Sayadhri Hills above Nasik in the extreme West to the Bay of Bengal in the East parallels the emerald Narmada which rises from Amarkantak in the far East and flows West to Gujarat into the Arabian Sea. It is inconceivable that two rivers running parallel to each other could flow a thousand miles in opposite directions. Yet Mother India is nothing if not inconceivable.

Shaped as the divine *yantra* of the inverse triangle, this ancient land is the fountainhead of all religions, the cradle of all culture and the motherland of all three races of man. The Devi Road, National Highway Seven, begins at the world's oldest city of Varanasi in the north, where the Goddess Anapurna, the "giver of food," dwells by the Ganges. The Devi Road runs over a thousand miles through Maihar in the center down to the country's tip at Kanya Kumari, the "virgin goddess." The Devi Road cleaves the *yantric* triangle of the sub-continent in twain.

CHAPTER SIX

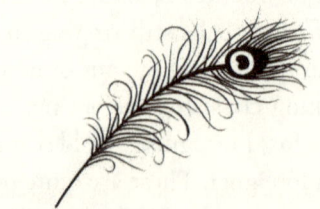

Discovering Parashurama Kunda
"The *Avatara* and the Axe"

kshatriya-rudhira-maye jagad-apagata-papam
snapayasi payasi samita-bhava-tapam
keshava dhrita-bhrgupati-rupa jaya jagadisha hare

"O Keshava! O Lord of the universe! O Lord Hari, who has assumed the form of Bhrigupati (Parashurama)! All glories to You! At Kurukshetra You bathe the earth in the rivers of blood from the bodies of the demoniac *kshatriyas* that You have slain. The sins of the world are washed away by You, and because of You people are relieved from the blazing fire of material existence." (Jayadeva Goswami)

THE ARYAN INVASION THEORY IMAGINES that India's lighter-skinned Northerners originated from the vicinity of Europe. It alleges that an entire civilization migrated en masse, completely displacing the earlier Dravidian culture, and drove it into the south, leaving behind no traces from whence it had come. Borrowing a well-known word from Sanskrit meaning "noble," the indologists called these new arrivals "Aryans," and thereby pitted the Northern Indians against the supposedly-relocated Dravidians of the South. Colonoialists thereby nailed a wedge between the people of India's north and south, in a diabolical and politically-motivated move of "divide and conquer."

There are several flaws to this fantastic Aryan invasion theory. First, no vast civilization has ever completely transplanted itself, leaving behind no traces from whence it came. Second, whenever mass migrations have occurred, resettlement always has resulted in a blending of cultures, and not a wholesale displacement of the previous inhabitants. Supposed evidence for the Aryan Invasion Theory is a linguistic one that traces similarities in language between India's Sanskrit and many of the so-called "Indo-European" languages."

The Vedic understanding of linguistic similarities reverses the Aryan invasion theory, because it concludes that the European civilization has actually descended from Vedic origins. Long before relatively modern names like "India" and "Hindu" were coined, what is now called India was known as Bharat. Thousands of years ago, there was an exodus of the warrior class from India that migrated to Europe to escape the wrath of a warrior god. This exodus from India explains not only the root similarities between many words in various European languages and Sanskrit, but it also explains parallels in religious culture between the pre-Christian so-called "Pagans" of Europe, and today's Hindu religion. The original indologists of the 18th Century like Sir William Jones concluded that Sanskrit is the oldest of all languages. In the same way, the eternal religion of the Sanskrit culture—or sanatana dharma—is the oldest of all religions.

The catalyst for the great migration out of ancient Bharata was an *avatara* of Lord Vishnu named Parashurama, or "Rama with the *parashu* (axe)." As told in *Srimad-Bhagavtam* (9.15.14), "Learned scholars accept this Parashurama as the celebrated incarnation of Vasudeva, who annihilated the dynasty of King Kartavirya. Parashurama killed all the *kshatriyas* on earth twenty-one times."

According to India's historical texts, the *Puranas*, Parashurama was so fierce and adept with his axe that he uprooted twenty-one generations of *kshatriyas*, or warriors. Those *kshatriyas* who were not killed by Parashurama in battle escaped and migrated westward. Eventually this warrior class created the great empires of Europe and the Mediterranean region from Egypt to Scandanavia to Great Britain. This explains not only similarities in language, but how the same deities that were worshiped in old Bharata are practically identical to the deities from the Near East, to Northern Africa, to Europe. For example the Vedic demigod of the Sun, Ravi, was worshiped throughout Europe. We are taught that there were a Greek sun god, a Roman sun god, or an Egyptian sun god. But common sense tells us that there is only one sun overhead, and that it has no interest in artificial boundaries made by men.

Today, there are still a few temples to Lord Parashurama in India. His worshipers understand that, since God is complete, and although He is a loving

God, His completeness must also include killing. A God who simply personifies love and kindness would be incomplete, and could therefore not be the Supreme Lord by the very definition of God. My Guru Maharaja made this point when discussing Parashurama, but he added that even when it is necessary, killing is not good. Therefore, Parashurama underwent a series of penance and auserities to counteract his "sin" of killing, although there can be no such thing as sin affecting the Supreme Lord or His *avataras*.

While traveling through central India, I learned that Parashurama performed *tapasya* in the Vindhya Hills, the low mountain range that roughly follows the Narmada River. Previously, I had bathed in the lakes of Kurushetra known as Samanta Panchaka, which were once the five lakes of the blood of warriors slaughtered by the axe of the *avatara*. I had once visited a Parashurama Temple in Uttarakashi in the Himalayas, where thie *avatara* had performed *yoga*. Now I became fascinated with the idea of finding the *tapo-bhumi* where he penanced after slaughtering twenty-one generations of *kshatriyas*. This idea stuck with me while hiking in the Vindhya Hills, once a towering mountain range whose great height had "the power to block the Sun."

According to Puranic tradition, these mountains had become hills when they bowed to the sage Atri, who had intervened on behalf of the Sun demigod. It is said that the Vindhyas were once very tall. As a favor to the Sun, Atri Muni asked the mountains to lower themselves so he could cross over them in his travels southward. He promised the Vindhyas that after he returned, they could again rise up. Subsequently, Atri Muni remained in the south—Dakshina Bharata—forcing the Vindhyas to appear more like a range of hills than mountains. However, today the gigantic boulders that adorn these hills speak of their once-great height. To this day, the Vindhya range is considered the dividing line between north and south India. The history of Lord Parashurama is told in the 9th canto of *Shrimad-Bhagavatam* as follows:

Once, millions of years ago, the great sage Richika approached Varuna, the demigod of waters. From Varuna, Richika obtained one thousand white horses as lustrous as moonlight, though each had one black ear. Richika Muni presented these horses to the great King Gadhi as dowry for his daughter, the beautiful and qualified Princess Satyavati. After her marriage, Satyavati longed to give her husband a son, so with prayers and appropriate *mantras*, Richika Muni created an oblation imbued with the powers of his *yogic siddhis*. By eating this divine preparation before procreative union with her husband, Satyavati's desires would be fulfilled. Richika had instilled the offering with *mantras* to produce a peaceful, forgiving *brahmana* who would be contented within himself.

However, King Gadhi's wife grew envious. The queen requested her son-in-law Richika to prepare a suitable oblation for her, too, since she also wanted a son. The muni agreed, but he injected her oblation with the powers to produce a *kshatriya* son, a bold and courageous prince willing to fight for truth and justice.

Once the two oblations were complete, the sage repaired to the river for his ritualistic bath. Meanwhile, the queen assumed that a husband would naturally place more potency into the preparation for his wife. Then, with her daughter's permission, the queen exchanged the two oblations and each lady honored the one meant for the other. When Richika Muni returned from his bath, he discovered the switch. Scolding his wife Satyavati, he said "You have acted wrongfully. Now because of that, your son will be a fierce *kshatriya* capable of punishing everyone. And your brother will be a scholar learned in all the spiritual sciences."

Satyavati was horrified and begged her husband to retract the effects. Thus pacified by her charm and devotion, Richika Muni then adjusted the reaction. "Since the *mantras* must take effect," he proclaimed, "therefore your grandson, rather than your son, will have an invincible *kshatriya* spirit." Thereafter, Satyavati became the mother of a great sage, the tolerant and austere Jamadagni, while her grandson became Lord Parashurama. *Shrimad-Bhagavtam* (1.3.20) states, "In the sixteenth incarnation of the Godhead, the Lord as Bhṛgupati (or Parashurama) annihilated the administrative class (*kshatriyas*) twenty-one times, being angry with them because of their rebellion against the brahmanas (the intelligent class)."

Long, long ago in the Treta Yuga, there was a great king named Kartavirya Arjuna. He had obtained the boon of having one thousand arms by worshiping the incarnation of Godhead Dattatreya. His vast opulence and mystic abilities only served to inflate his ego. Once Kartavirya Arjuna was sporting in the Narmada River in the company of many beautiful young ladies. This place sat alongside his capital of Mahishmatipura, which today is called Mandla, and lies around an hour and a half south of Jabalpur. To demonstrate his prowess before the admiring young ladies, King Kartavirya Arjuna dammed the Narmada River's flow with his one thousand arms. Upstream, where the demonic King Ravana had halted with his army, the river breached its banks and flooded his encampment. Furious, the mighty Ravana challenged Kartavirya over the insult, although he would prove to be no match for him. The thousand-armed king captured Ravana, and then neglectfully set him free as one might catch and release a monkey. Now Kartavirya Arjuna considered himself practically invinceable.

Some time after this incident, King Kartavirya Arjuna traveled north where he met Sage Jamadagni at his forest hermitage. With the help of his splendid *kamadhenu*, a celestial wish-fulfilling cow, Jamadagni sumptupusly fed the king and his vast retinue. But Kartavirya Arjuna grew envious, He could not tolerate that a mere sage could own anything that surpassed his opulence, and he ordered his men to steal the cow along with her calf. After all, he reasoned, the king must hve the best of everything. Kartivirya then took the weeping *kamadhenu* to his capital at Mahishmatipura.

Upon hearing of the great offense, Parashurama, the son of Jamadagni, became as angry as a trampled snake. Though born of a sage, Parashurama was influenced by the *kshatriya* oblations as predicted by his grandfather Richika Muni. These activities of the Lord's *avatara*'s are taken as divine *lila*, or pastimes, since Krishna and His incarnaions are never touched by the actions of material nature. His pastimes in various incarnations are meant to attract different souls into his *lila* in order to free them from the ocean of birth and death.

Parashurama took up his axe, shield and bow and arrows, and pursued Kartavirya just as a lion chases an elephant. When the king saw the angry sage approaching, he gasped in fear. He sent his huge army of hundreds of thousands of soldiers to punish Parashurama, but the Lord easily slaughtered the lot of them by rushing here and there "as swiftly as the mind." The battleground turned to mud due to the blood spilling from the headless and limbless torsoes of slain warriors.

At that time, the courageous Kartavirya decided to personally confront the sixteenth incarnation of God on the field of battle. Taking up five hundred bows fixed with five hundred arrows, he issued a challenge. Yet, with just a single bow, the Lord cut to pieces each of the king's weapons. Furious, the thousand-armed king uprooted trees and rushed at Parashurama intent on killing him. With great force and agility, Parashurama cut off each of the king's thousand arms, and then beheaded him, sending him to follow his troops to a grisly doom. As the ten thousand sons of the king witnessed their father's death, they ran away in fear. Parashurama then gently released the stolen *kamadhenu* and her calf, and returned them to the *ashram* of his father Jamadagni.

As explained in the *Bhagavata* (9.15.38-40), after bowing before his father, and greeting his brothers, the warrior sage explained every detail of the battle including the heroic death of Kartavirya. Still, the tolerant and gentle Jamadagni scolded his son. "Oh great hero," he began, "You have unnecessarily killed the king, who is supposed to be the embodiment of all the demigods. Thus you have committed a sin. We brahmanas are worshiped only due to our quality of forgiveness, which is illuminating like the sun. It is only through his quality of forebearance that Lord Brahma has achieved the post of supreme spiritual master of the entire universe. The Supreme Personality of Godhead, the all-pervasive Hari, becomes pleased with those who are forgiving, for cultivation of this quality is a *brahmana's* duty."

Rishi Jamadagni then instructed Parashurama to observe penance in the form of *tirtha-samsevaya*—visiting holy places—to atone for his misdeed. He explained: "My dear son, killing a king who is an emperor is more severely sinful than killing a *brahmana*. But now, if you become Krishna conscious and worship the holy places, you can atone for this great sin." (SB 9.15.41) With that, Parashurama left for *tirtha-yatra*, visiting holy cities, *ashrams* of great sages, rivers, lakes, hills and mountains throughout Bharata. In truth, Lord Parashurama had committed no sin in the execution of his divine *lila*. In fact, the very warriors he slaughtered received liberation, having been killed by an incarnation of the Supreme Lord Vishnu or Hari. The places of pilgrimage that he visited were themselves actually blessed by his lotus feet.

Still, in order to teach that killing is generally uncalled for except in extreme instances, Sage Jamadagni ordered *tirtha-sevaya* to his son: "Go and serve the holy places." Most pilgrims visit sacred shrines and rivers just to bathe and to wash away any lingering effects of past sins. Yet, the actual purpose of *tirtha-sevaya* is to associate with holy devotees of the Lord, who reside at these places for the sake of human welfare. Therefore, Lord Parashurama's example of obedience to his father is exemplary. He replied, *tatha iti*: "Let it be so." He then undertook a tour of Bharata's sacred *punya-bhumis* for a full year of blessing the sub-continent, after which he returned to the *ashram* of his family.

Meanwhile, the miserable sons of Kartavirya had been nursing a grudge against Parashurama since the death of their father. One day, while Parashurama was roaming in the woods with his brothers, the vengeful sons of Kartavirya Arjuna invaded their hermitage where Jamadagni was seated in *yogic* trance. Renuka begged them not to harm her husband, a gentle *brahmana* who was absorbed in meditation upon the Supreme Absolute Truth. Yet, from their point of view, had not Parashurama deprived them of their father? Now, along with his brothers he would understand the meaning of such a loss. Being devoid of noble *kshatriya* qualities, they beheaded the sage in front of his wife and absconded with his head.

Deep in the forest, the boys heard the cries of Renuka shouting, "O Rama! O Rama!" Rushing to the *ashram*, the brothers found their mother crying hysterically and beating her bosom in anguish. Parashurama saw that she beat her chest twenty-one times, and with that he vowed to rid the world of mischievous *kshatriyas* for twenty-one generations. Parashurama immediately began for Mahishmati, a city that was doomed due to the murder of a *brahmana*. There, the sage-warrior extracted a terrible toll by creating a mountain of ten thousand heads of the princes, just as they had beheaded his father. When other memebrs of the kingly class saw the rivers of blood, they trembled in fear.

Lord Parashurama located the head of his father, and returned to the *ashram* with it. There, with the power of his mystic *siddhis* and divine *mantras*, he secured the head to the body of his father, which had been preserved by his brothers. Then, by the miraculous touch of the Lord, Jamadagni returned to life as if waking from a deep sleep. Afterward, the all-victorious Parashurama completed his vow by taking his ritualistic bath in the Saraswati River.

After ridding the earth twenty-one times of the burden of defiant *kshatriyas*, who were maddened by lust for power, Parashurama came here to penance in the region of the Narmada and the Vindhyas. Today, the Vindhyas are revered only second to the Himalayas. Although Parashurama's *lila* occurred millions of years ago during the Treta Yuga, he is still said to be living upon this earth. He is one of the few *chiranjivis*, who can live in the same body for as long as the earth itself shall exist.

One day, while hiking in the Vindhya Hills near Jabalpur, I encountered an English-speaking *sadhu* by the will of Providence. He was familiar with the location of Parashurama's *tapo-bhumi*. He said, "Parashurama Kunda is in nearby Khamaria, here in the Jabalpur District. The *kunda* itself is within the Pariat River. The area is part farmland and part jungle inhabited by adivasi tribals. Nearby is a hill called Parashurama Giri, upon which there is a rock imprinted with the *avatara*'s footwear." As I thanked the *sadhu* for the information, he responded with the holy name of the Lord, "Rama, Rama," and went on his way disappearing behind the huge boulders.

The next day, a friend of mine and I decided to find the *kunda*. Gyan Prakash cranked up his old India-build Lambretta scooter, and I got on the Enfield. The way to the *kunda* would be through jungle paths of sun-baked earth, which are easily navigated for a motorcycle that weighs only 375 pounds.

As we turn off Highway 22 at Khamaria, we pass through the village of Matamar, which consists only of a few mud and straw huts. There, an old villager singing bhajans beneath a shade tree points in the direction of Parashurama Kunda, about a mile away. Beyond the village are settlements of Gond tribals, who live either by fishing and hunting, or by working menial jobs that pay a day wage. These Gonds have their own primitive religion, language and customs that separate them from the mainstream Hindus. Indeed, their languages and customs vary from tribe to tribe.

We find our way through the fields and jungle paths until we are overlooking a *kunda* that is surrounded by the huge tantaniya boulders that decorate the Vindhya range. These gigantic rocks are named for the sound that emanates from them when the wind blows around them. Rising up half a kilometer beyond the *kunda* is the large, isolated Parashurama Giri, the hill of the *avatara*, where a stone marked by his footprints sits in secrecy. Alongside the *kunda* is a tiny, yet rare and somewhat desolate, Parashurama Mandir.

Near the edge of the *kunda* is a straw hut, and alongside the hut is a small field where vegetables are grown. From the hut emerges a *yogi* dressed in a rough orange cloth, resembling burlap. Renunciates often wear the cloth of old burlap bags and call it "the last cloth." This means that it is the last cloth that anyone would ever want to wear. Such an austere garment is a mark of their renunciation away from the finery of this world. We greet the *yogi* with folded hands. As I bow before him, he makes a sound like phhht, and strikes me hard on the back with his fist, as both a test of my tolerance and as a blessing. As he eyes me curiously to examine my reaction, I thank him with the words, "Dhanyavad, Babaji,"

We are surprised that he speaks English. He was once Shri M.K. Rana, born in Nepal, and who worked as a policeman here in Jabalpur District until his sixties. Rather than retire to the care of his family, he tells us that Lord Parashurama has called him to care for the his holy bathing place. He has now become Mahankala *Baba*, named for Lord Shiva, "the lord of time."

Mahankala Babaji offers us some pieces of coconut which Gyan Prakash and I accept respectfully, although we don't eat it right away. We are not sure whether he is a scheming tantric who might have mixed dhatura poison with food offerings in order to waylay tourists. Such wicked *yogis* are still quite common in many areas of India. Indeed, at many tourist areas to this day you will see signs reading, "Do not accept food from strangers." Politely, we explain that we need to bathe in the *kunda* before honoring *prasada*. After prayers and Gayatri meditation, we enter the small lake.

The waters of Parashurama Kund are refreshing to the spirit. After about fifteen minutes, I notice a dark-skinned Gond tribal observing us, squatting timidly behind some tall grasses. Keeping him the corner of my eye, I pretend not to notice. He is obviously merely curious, and is no threat to our safety. Having taken my sacred dip, I emerge from the waters slowly and dress, keeping the tribal in the corner of my eye while donning my clothes. There is a trick in

India never to completely undress in front of anyone by covering wet garments with dry ones. The technique is to simultaneously drop the wet clothes, while putting on the dry ones. Soon I wring out the wet garments in the *kunda* and drape them over the handlebars to dry. That done, I let the tribal know that he has been seen by offering a casual yet polite salute with folded hands in his direction. He continues to gaze from behind tall grasses without responding to the gesture.

The Gonds have their own primitive religion, and the Hindu methods of offering respect apparently are not part of it. He continues staring at Gyan as I head towards the little shrine. The Deity is a carved stone figure of Lord Parashurama. His parashu rests upon his shoulder, and he offers blessings with the palm of his right hand in the abhaya mudra. By its design, it appears that the Deity is over one hundred years old. After some minutes of prayerful *mantras*, we pay a visit to Mahankal Babaji at his hut. One clue that he is trustworthy is that he knows the area quite well. Villainous tantrics seldom stay in any place for very long out of fear for their lives at the hands of angry villagers. Finally, in Babaji's presence we honor the coconut prasad that he gave us earlier.

Pointing to the direction of the village that we passed through, Babaji tells us that some local industry is eyeing property rights to dig up the *tirtha* in order to manufacture bricks from the clay-rich soil. His duty, he emphasizes, has been given to him by Lord Parashrurama to preserve his *tapo-bhumi*. He poses the question, "If I do not prevent them from desecrating the sacred ground of the Lord's *tirtha*, then who will?"

I inquire whether any other foreigners have visited this place, and he replies with a friendly giggle, "Are you kidding? Even the locals don't know about it." He explains that there is a small festival held here once a year on Makara Sankranti in mid-January when the Sun enters Capricorn, or Makara rashi. That is the moment when the Sun demigod begins his six-month northward trek, or uttarayana, as days gradually become longer. He says that there is no other mela held here, and only a handful of folks from the surrounding villages attend. When I asked him about the pada-shila, or rock bearing the footprints of Lord Parashurama, he admonishes us that is has been seen only by a rare few, daring us to find it and hinting that we will not.

Now it has grown late in the day, so I promise myself that I will return again soon and take up the search. During subsequent visits, I was able to find an alternate route via the Panagar Road by which the *kunda* can be approached from the right side of the Pariat stream. On that side of the hill a one-legged *yogi* lives in a cave near the ruins of a once-great acnient temple. The *yogi* is maintained by villagers who daily supply him with food.

The history ot the old temple, whose great, broken pillars lie half-submerged in the earth, is shrouded in the myteries of time, although it was likely a great temple to Parashurama. Since ancient times, it has has been the custom to erect temples at the site of the activities of the various *avataras*, demigods as well as to the Supeme Lord Vishnu or Krishna Himself. Central India, or Gondwana, was conquered by the Mughals of Delhi when they defeated the Hindu Queen Durgavati in 1564. Rani Durgavati, who commanded an army of trained Gond tribals, was killed upon her elephant mount in battle some twenty-five miles to the south of here. Later, in the 1600's, Akbar's intolerant son Aurangzeb wreaked havoc upon this region with his policy of temple desecration and destruction. This is the most plausible explanation for these ruins.

Today in India there is no large temple to Lord Parashurama. Parashurama Kunda at Khamaria, Jabalpur District, would make an ideal location for one since the axe-wielding *avatara* is still believed to perform penance at this very spot. With the patronage of a single wealthy businessman, a magnificent temple to Parashurama could arise again here for the glory of Moher India and the world. Thousands of pilgrims travel this route each month to visit the Hill of Devi where Sharada Maa is worshiped a few hours north at Maihar. Each tourist vehicle would certainly include this spot in their itinerary. The lost jungle shrine of the empowered incarnation Lord Parashurama could be turned into a place of pilgrimage once again, before horrendous industries and the urban sprawl of apartment complexes encroach upon a spiritual treasure. Which will arrive first—the pious pilgrims or the bulldozers?

Though I have returned several times, I have yet to see the Lord's footprints in the sacred shila atop Parashurama Giri. Yet the Enfield found its finest hour in the "discovery" of Parashurama Kunda, for without this rugged bike I would never have found the hidden *tapo-bhumi* of the axe-wielding *avatara*.

CHAPTER SEVEN

The Ride to Rama Giri
"Lord Rama's Weapons"

*vitarasi dikshu rane dik-pati-kamaniyam
dasa-mukha-mauli-balim ramaniyam
keshava dhrta-rama-sarira jaya jagadisha hare*

O Keshava! O Lord of the universe! O Lord Hari, who has assumed the form of Ramachandra! All glories to You! In the battle of Lanka You destroy the ten-headed demon Ravana and distribute his heads as a delightful offering to the presiding deities of the ten directions, headed by Indra. This action was long desired by all of them, who were much harassed by this monster. (Jayadeva Goswami)

"I FIRST SAW RAMA GIRI BEFORE YOU WERE BORN," I say, boasting to my young Sikh friend Anukaran, trying to stir his interest to visit the hill (*giri*) of Lord Ramacandra with me.

"I've never been there," he replies, "although I was born just thirty miles away in Nagpur."

"So why don't we ride up there tomorrow? We can take the Enfields."

"Let's get an early start," he says, accepting the invitation. "I can leave at nine."

Anukaran Singh was born in a wealthy Indian family, descendants of proud Punjabi Sikh warriors who generation after generation have laid down their lives against successive waves of tyrannical invaders. Despite his involvement with his family's business, Anukaran is frank about wanting to reestablish his link with India's ancient heritage, the birthright of anyone born in this vast and diverse land.

"In the 70s, it was the fashion to be ignorant of our civilization and culture," Anukaran jokes. "For my present generation, it is the fashion to know more about our actual heritage."

It will be our privilege to journey to the sacred hill where the Personality of Godhead Lord Rama, His wife and queen, Sita Devi, and younger brother Laksmana were received by the great ascetic Agastya Muni. Ever since that memorable hilltop meeting, the Agastya *ashram* has been honored by pilgrims as Rama Giri.

Millions of years ago in the age called Treta-*yuga*, the Supreme Personality of Godhead Lord Sri Krishna descended as a king: Lord Rama, or Ramachandra. Lord Ramacandra's adventures or *lilas* were written down by the *adika-vi* ("first poet") Valmiki Muni. *Valmiki* literally means "he who has emerged from an anthill." By meditating on Lord Rama's transcendental *lila*, Valmiki became so steadfastly absorbed in the *yoga* of spiritual trance that huge jungle ants were able to build a hill around him. After many years, he emerged from the anthill to scribe the 24,000-verse Sanskrit scripture *Ramayana*, the world's oldest book.

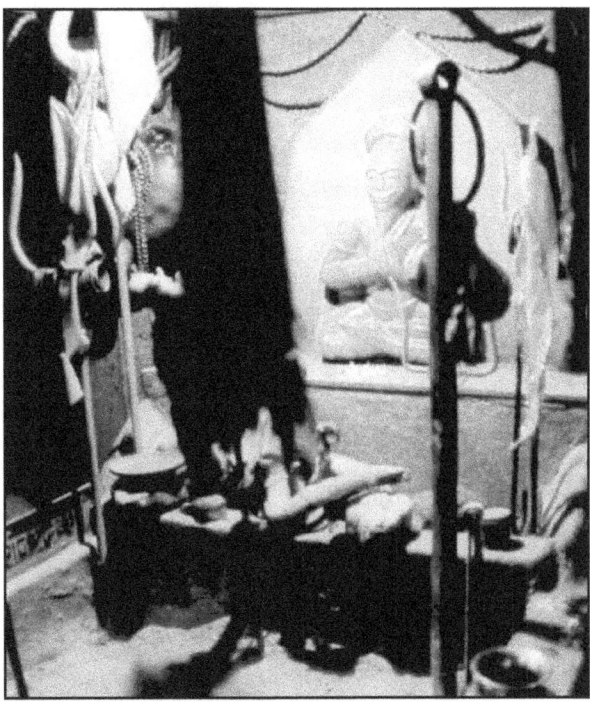

Deity of Agastya at Rama Giri

The purpose of Lord Rama's advent is to attract us conditioned souls to the timeless, transcendental path of *bhakti-yoga,* devotional service. By reading the Lord's pastimes in the *Srimad-Bhagavatam* or in the *Ramayana,* and by hearing of His exceptional prowess from the lips of pure devotees like my Guru Maharaja Srila Prabhupada, even the unsophisticated soul becomes drawn to the blissful security of genuine spiritual life. If a pilgrimage is undertaken in a spirit of remembrance of the Lord's *lila,* then visiting the holy places connected with His pastimes can be purifying and uplifting, in the all-important quest for inner development

Since time immemorial, each of us embodied *jiva* souls has been revolving through the grim cycle of rebirth called *samsara*. To deliver His servants trapped in the net of *maya,* God comes Himself or sends His *avatara* for our salvation from the delusion of material ignorance. Attraction to the lotus feet of the Lord, acceptance of His divine shelter, and the joyful singing of His name open the door for going back home, back to Godhead.

To this day, millions of years after the advent of Sita-Rama, their Their followers number in the hundreds of millions. The supreme royal couple is even worshiped outside India. In Thailand, for example, a quarter-mile stretch of the halls of the royal palace is artistically painted with scenes from the *Ramayana*. In the island of Bali in Indonesia, and also in Cambodia and Nepal, thousands more Rama temples can be found. In every corner of India, from tiny village shrines to fabulous temple palaces, the transcendental form of Lord Rama is worshiped, and His all-liberating name is sung by His devotees.

According to Valmiki's *Ramayana,* Sri Rama, on the order of His father, King Dasaratha, left His hometown of Ayodhya (in present-day Uttar Pradesh) and embraced forest life. "As the full moon enters a cloud bank," Rama, Sita, and Laksmana wandered south through the woods to the mountain Chitrakuta. From there they wended their way into Madhya Bharata (central India), hiking through the valleys of the holy Vindhya Hills and crossing the sacred Narmada River. Then they came to the vast Dandaka Forest, the abode of hermits. As Prabhupada teaches, when Lord Rama passed through the Dandaka Forest, many sages achieved perfection in *yoga* just by seeing Him. Their dormant love of Godhead became awakened, According to *Padma Purana*, these fortunate *rishis* were later reborn as *gopis* (cowherd girls) in the *lila* of Lord Sri Krsna, the original Supreme Personality of Godhead.

Rama, Sita and Lakshmana camped here and there, bravely bearing the hardships of jungle life, and finally arrived at the *ashram* of Agastya Muni, atop what is now called Rama Giri. As a king, a member of the *kshatriya* class, Lord

Rama offered His respects to the *brahmana* Agastya Muni with sweet words. The Lord feels so grateful to His devotees that He bows before them.

The incomparable Agastya Muni was *tri-kala-jna:* He could see the three features of time—past, present, and future. Hence, he was well aware that Sri Rama is none other than the almighty Visnu Himself, and that in the very near future He would fight a great war with the enemies of *dharma*, the demons (*asuras*).

Many sages of the Dandaka Forest had already suffered grievous harassment at the hands of atheistic *asuras,* and many had fallen victim to their evil schemes. Yet, try as they might, none of these *asuras* could trap the wily Agastya. Through his unbreakable penance and high intelligence, the sage had even outwitted the evil duo Ilvala and Vatapi. Ilvala, taking the form of a Sanskrit-speaking *brahmana,* would invite different sages to share a meal. Then Vatapi would assume the form of the meal. After dinner Ilvala would smile and say, "Come out, Vatapi," and Vatapi would suddenly burst forth, splitting the poor *rishi's* belly.

Once Agastya, as requested by the *devas* or demigods, accepted Ilvala's invitation to dine with him. After the meal, the grinning Ilvala called for his wicked brother to exit the sage's body.But Agastya smiled and declared, "Your brother cannot come out now because he has already been sent to the abode of Yamaraja, the Lord of death, by the fire of my digestion." The infuriated Ilvala sprang forward, rushing at Agastya, but one stern and fiery look from the powerful sage reduced him to ashes in an instant.

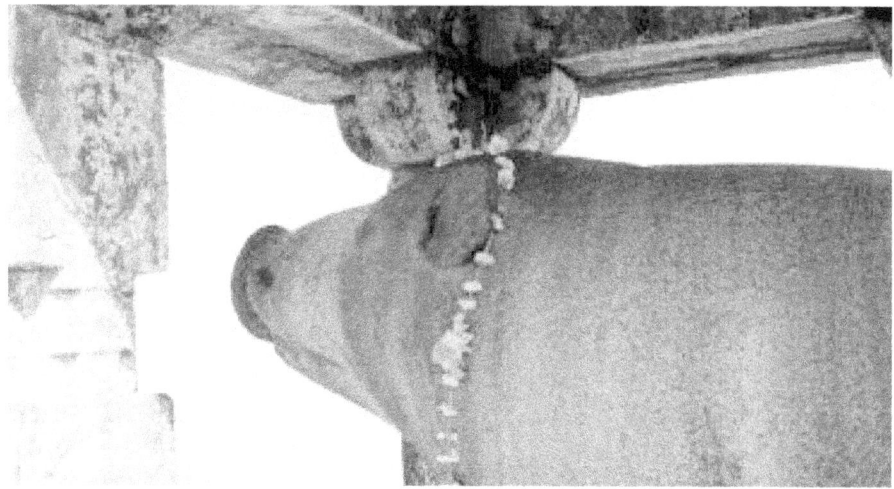

As told earlier in our description of Parashurama Kunda, the diminutive Agastya once requested the Vindhya Mountains to bow low, because their towering peaks were blocking the sun. Agastya promised the lord of the Vindhyas that his rolling hills could rise up and become mountains again once he returned from the south. To keep the Vindhyas humble, Agastya never returned north again. Instead, he made his hermitage here at Rama Giri, in the Deccan, south of the Vindhyas.

Saint Agastya received Sita, Rama, and Laksmana with customary offerings of fruit and flowers. Then he presented Lord Rama with the Brahma-datta bow, which Lord Indra had earlier entrusted to his care. The bow had been inset with diamonds by its creator, Visvakarma, the engineer of the universe. Along with the bow, Agastya handed over to Sri Rama a quiver of arrows that included the undefeatable *brahmashtra* weapon. He also presented Lord Ramacandra with a sword in a jeweled scabbard. Rama took a vow to vanquish the trouble-making demons, and as He did so, Rama Giri shook.

By accepting the weapons from Agastya, the Lord displayed His intention of protecting His devotees. Today the village at the foot of Rama Giri is called Rama Tek, literally "Rama's vow." In *Bhagavad-gita* (4.7-8) Lord Krsna explains His vow to shelter His devotees: "Whenever and wherever there is a decline in religious practice, O descendant of Bharata, and a predominant rise of irreligion at that time I descend Myself. To deliver the pious and to annihilate the miscreants, as well as to reestablish the principles of religion, I Myself appear, millennium after millennium."

Much later at Sri Lanka, during the battle with Ravana and his demonic hoard, Sri Rama's charioteer, Matali, was to remind Rama of the weapons presented by Agastya Muni. True to Agastya's vision and Rama's promise, Rama fired the arrow imbued with *brahmashtra mantras* into the heart of Ravana, where the demon had stored *amrta,* the nectar of deathlessness. It is the Lord's promise to protect His devotees, and He does so in every age.

ॐ ॐ ॐ

At 9:00 the next morning, Anukaran pulls up and revs his engine, and I rush out and kick-start my Enfield Bullet.

"Let's get going," I advise him. "The auspicious time for departure lasts for only another fifteen minutes." Within seconds we are headed north to Rama Giri.

After an hour of country riding, sunburned and smiling, we see the hill of Lord Rama off to our right. Leaning east, we ride through Ram Tek village, with its unusual collection of shops, *ashrams, dharmshalas* (pilgrim's rest houses), and Buddhist Ayurvedic *ashrams*.

Riding through the narrow lanes of merchants and farm animals, we find ourselves at last on the twisting road up the hill to the peak of Rama Giri. About half way to the top, we slow down to pass a group of several dozen *pada-yatris,* "pilgrims who go by foot." Judging by the *dhoti*-like way the women have tied their saris, I guess they are a group of Maharastrian villagers. Some walk barefoot, not for want of shoes, but for the higher merit accrued for the austerity.

As the last curve of the road widened to the top, we find ourselves before the steep rock wall of Rama Giri fort. The fort was built several centuries ago by kings of the Bhonsle clan. Rama Giri was chosen as the fort's site for two reasons: First, the hill strategically offers a 360-degree view of the surrounding area, which it was the kings' duty to protect, Secondly, Vedic kings, even as late as the eighteenth century, were impelled by their religious convictions to guard holy areas. In 1827, however, after the Bhonsle warriors suffered defeat at the hands of British invaders at the Battle of Sitalbuldi, their reign over the area rapidly deteriorated. Today the fort with its old tanks and temples is a protected monument, a historical oddity frozen in time.

After parking the Enfields, we offer our respect to the huge, rare deity of Lord Visnu-Varaha, who overlooks the valley and the fort. This is one of two giant Varaha deities weighing several tons that I know of. Deities of the Lord's boar incarnation are rare. There are two ancient Varaha temples in Mathura that were visited by Lord Sri Chaitanya Mahaprabhu, as documented in *Shri Chaitanya-charitamrta*. Another white marble deity of Lord Varaha is worshiped in a temple along the shores of Pushkar Lake in Rajasthan. But the only other deity of Lord Varaha this large is the *svayam-bhu* ("self-manifested") Sri Visnu-Varahaji of Majholi, Madhya Pradesh. After garlanding Lord Varaha and receiving *prasadam* from the priest, Anukaran and I enter the *ashram* of Agastya Muni.

Lavishly preserved in marble and carefully maintained by a group of *sadhus,* the hermitage has been developed as a pilgrims' destination of much importance. Even the *yajna-shala,* the holy place of fire sacrifices where the *rsi* received Lord Rama, has been continuously maintained since Treta-*yuga*. An iron door has been installed over Agastya's deep cave; only select *yogis* are allowed entrance into the chamber, called Hatiphor. The *ashram's* astute crew of ascetics display extreme care in the upkeep and worship of Saint Agastya's shrine.

Beyond Agastya Muni's peaceful cave is a large group of temples, the first of which is dedicated to Lakshmana, who led the way to Rama Giri. It was Lakshmana who announced to the sages the arrival of his brother Rama and sister-in-law Sita. This explains why the Laksmana Mandir is first. The other temples are separately dedicated to Lord Rama, Goddess Sita, and Bhakta Hanuman.

The local history of the Deities is noteworthy. In 1736 King Raghu Bhonsle visited Rama Giri, only to discover that just the *padukas,* or wooden sandals of Lord Rama, were being worshiped there. The Deities were no longer present. The king vowed to commission Jaipur Deities for the temple. But once the sacred *murtis* were prepared for the temple installation, or *prana-pratistha,* the king had a dream in which Lord Rama told him to search under the waters of the River Sur a few miles north. Finally, in 1753, the original Deities were discovered exactly as revealed in the king's dream, and They were re-installed atop Rama Giri amidst much festivity. The Jaipur Deities are privately cared for in a reserved area.

Anukaran and I linger at each temple, offering whatever rupees we have to spare. After *darsana,* we climbed up the steps to the top of the fortress wall to view the vast valley of farmland, lakes, and tiny villages encircling Rama Giri. Gently at first, the sound of *kirtana,* the *yuga-dharma* of chanting of the Lord's holy name, wafts up from the temple room, accompanied by the ringing of *karatalas* (hand cymbals). The *pada-yatri* pilgrims we had passed on the road are now sitting peacefully before Lord Rama's Deity, singing His holy names. Now every face within earshot reflects blissful meditation upon God.

Struck by the serenity of Lord Rama's temple on Rama Giri, I take advantage of the uplifted mood to speak what I have learned from my Guru Maharaja. "Anukaran," I begin, "the worship of Lord Rama or Lord Shri Krishna is universal, and is not intended only for some particular sect or religion. Their names are imbued with the potency to deliver anyone, any living entity, from every misery into the unlimited world of transcendental bliss. The name of the Lord is nondifferent from the person of the Lord Himself. Although He is the master of the personal spiritual worlds, inhabited by liberated souls who are absorbed in His loving service, He descends to our world for our deliverance. His worship is performed best in the Kali-*yuga* by the chanting of His name, a means open to members of all races and religions. The *sankirtana* movement that Shrila Prabhupada introduced to the entire world is essentially the same as the melodic vibrations which we are savoring even now.

"Lord Rama never fancied Himself to be some Hindu God. He is none other than the all-pervasive Vishnu, the Lord of the universe, and this is accepted as such by sages like Agastya. See how Hanuman and his army of *vanaras* (monkeys), as well as jungle bears and even a squirrel, were impelled to offer their service unto Sri Rama, never considering any selfish rewards. You must be aware your fourth Sikh *guru* was named Guru Ramadas, 'servant of Rama.'

"Just as worship of Lord Rama or Vishnu is uplifting and spiritually invigorating, so is the chanting of Their holy names. Lord Shri Chaitanya Mahaprabhu often quoted a verse from the *Brhan-Naradiya Purana:*

> *harer nama harer nama harer namaiva kevalam*
> *kalau nasty eva nasty eva nasty eva gatir anyatha*

The holy name! The holy name! The holy name! In this iron age called Kali-*yuga* there is no other way, no other way, no other way to reach the goal"

"In fact, quite along these lines your *Guru Granth Sahib,* which I once spent a week at Amritsar studying, plainly advises: 'The name of the Lord Hari destroys all miseries and purifies sinners, O beloved ... Through service to Sri Hari is the highest platform achieved.

... The name of Sri Hari is the highest benediction in Kali-*yuga*.' (Raga Asa, Mahala IV, Ghar II.1-2)

"In Kali-*yuga* the name of Rama is the boat that ferries the disciple. In this world, and in the next, the disciple of the *guru* lives in bliss by the grace of the name of Rama.

"Guru Nanak advises, 'Having heard the name of Lord Rama, we have become absorbed with love of God ... The name of Rama pleases the chanter's mind, and he achieves supreme happiness. He for whom the chanting of the name of Rama is a constant companion, even when leaving this world he never goes to the world of Yamaraja. O brother, I meditate on Lord Rama.'" (Raga Asa IV, Ghar I, Chant II, IX. 1, 2.3)

We fall into silence as our attention now drifts to the pristine beauty of the sacred lake below, Ambala Kund. Around the still waters of the lake, temples and shade trees dot the shore. The lake is said to have been named for King Amba, who was cured of a terrible disease after his bath in these waters, which originate from an underground river called Patala Ganga. In the eighteenth century King Raghu Bhonsle fortified the lake and renovated many of the shore temples with fine stone work. These temples include those of Jagannatha, Panchamukhi Mahadeva ("five-faced Shiva"), and Surya Narayana (the Sun god incarnation of Lord Vishnu).

Carried more by spiritual energy than reason at this point, Anukaran and I find ourselves in the saddles of the Enfields, riding downhill toward Ambala Kund. Finding a shady spot, we pull over. The noonday sun overhead tells me it is time for Gayatri meditation.

Much later, after returning to the States, I find this message in my mail box: "The other members of the Enfield Club are eager to visit Rama Giri on our next ride. Hare Krishna. Anukaran."

※ ※ ※

In his poetic translation of *Ramayana*, Sri Romesh Chunder Dutt, a nineteenth-century Vaisnava poet from Bengal, described Ravana's last moments, and the joy of victory felt by Lord Rama's army:

Pike and club and mace and trident scaped from Ravan's vengeful hand,
Spear and arrows Rama wielded, and his bright and flaming brand!

Long and dubious battle lasted, shook the ocean, hill and dale,
Winds were hushed in voiceless terror and the livid sun was pale,

Still the dubious battle lasted, until Rama in his ire
Wielded Brahma's deathful weapon flaming with celestial fire!

Weapon which the Saint Agastya had unto the hero given,
Winged as lightning dart of Indra, fatal as the bolt of heaven,

Wrapped in smoke and flaming flashes, speeding from the circled bow,
Pierced the iron heart of Ravan, lain the lifeless hero low,

And a cry of pain and terror from the Raksha ranks arose,
And a shout from joying Vanars as they smote their fleeing foes!

Heavenly flowers in rain descended on the red and gory plain,
And from unseen harps and timbrels rose a soft celestial strain,

And the ocean heaved in gladness, brighter shone the sunlit sky,
Soft and cool the gentle zephyrs through the forest murmured by,

Sweetest scent and fragrant odours wafted from celestial trees,
Fell upon the earth and ocean, rode upon the laden breeze!

Voice of blessing from the bright sky fell on Raghu's valiant son,
"Champion of the true and righteous! Now thy noble task is done!"

CHAPTER EIGHT

At a Stoplight in Nagpur
"A Moment to Reflect"

NAGPUR, IN THE STATE OF MAHARASHTRA, is a huge sprawling middle-of-nowhere megalopolis at the crossroads of Central India, right in the heart of the other side of the world. If you were to mark an "X" Delhi to Madras, and Calcutta to Bombay, Nagpur would fall right at the crux. It is India's hot spot, sweltering in the sub-continent's central plains with summertime temperatures sometimes rising above 120 degrees (F). Once a forested area of serpent worshipping Gond tribals, Nagpur literally means, "snake town."

The British arrived here in the 1820's and with little ado wrenched power from the ruling Marathas, the Marathi-speaking Bhonsle kings. After emerging victorious at the Battle of Sitalbuldi in 1827, the new British rulers built the fort atop Nagpur's highest hill and surveyed their empire. That old fort, today home to the India Army's Grenadier—or commando—division, now enjoys a 180-degree view of endless third world urban sprawl. Here the Grenadiers respectfully tend to the graves where their ancient enemies lie buried. This is remarkable since the Vedic civilization has for aeons cremated its dead. Yet for the Hindu *kshatriya* or warrior, it is a sacred duty to honor the worthy enemy, in life or death, even to the point of following traditions not his own.

Right here at the crossroads of India, samsara, or life's ever-turning wheel, has been momentarily riveted by a red light. Straddling a 1980 twin pipe single 250cc Yezdi, India's version of the two-stroke Jawa "Californian," I stand at the line frozen in time bombarded by the impatient sounds of jammed traffic all about me. Drowned by the beeping horns of drivers who think that honking will make the light turn green; the angry noises of the larger vehicles, trucks and buses; the commands of farmers to their oxen; the little arguments among other two-wheelers who vie for space, this is a spring-loaded waiting game. Here he whose mind is fixed upon the task at hand can alone survive.

The Jawa motorcycle like the one I am riding came to India from Czechoslovakia in the early 1960's. It evolved into the Yezdi in the mid-70's and unfortunately ceased production with the Japanese invasion by the big four (Honda, Kawasaki, Suzuki and Yamaha) in the mid-80's. Despite the fact that the Yezdi factory closed down shop some decade and a half-ago, used specimens are still common. Today a solid Jawa or Yezdi can be purchased and entirely rebuilt with durable new paint for around $600, a real bargain for a practically new bike capable of negotiating 100,000 thrilling kilometers of mountain, jungle and desert terrain. My Yezdi is the perfect Third World-mobile, responsive, quick and simple to ride ... or would be if the light would turn green.

Before me, the lop-sided and soot-encrusted red light that has obliged me to halt looks as though it must have been dangling here before the first motorized vehicle ever came to India. In fact, the traffic signal is a relatively new imposition upon Nagpur's crowded intersections. I seriously doubt that any of the bicycles, bullock carts, pedal and motor rickshaws, scooters, mini-cars and mini-vans, imitation 4X4's, trucks and buses would have halted for a mere dangling light if it were not for a snarling, dark-complexioned, brown-uniformed policeman standing grimly in the center of the crossroads. A gang of his fellow cops, obviously his seniors, their dark, sweaty brows furled to disguise the fact that they are loafing, huddle together off to the side. Doubtless their presence insures the honesty of the impatient motorists, and helps guarantee the safety of their junior colleague facing off precariously before tensely spring-loaded rows of chaotic traffic from hell.

Police here can look more taciturn, threatening and tough than the thugs they are underpaid to control. Though I have counted many cops among my friends in India, due to necessity, curiosity or genuine respect, I am not especially well disposed towards Nagpur's men of the uniform at this particular junction. Ten minutes ago a menacing group of Nagpur's finest formed a human barricade across the road and forced me to pull over. My international driving license kept my bike and me out of their clutches, but there was one detail that had to be sorted out. The cop pointed to the lane in which I was blissfully moving along, minding my own business, and said, "One way."

"No sign!?" I responded quickly, looking around at others moving in the same wrong direction.

"Yes, no sign. You pay 150 rupees."

I answered, "Correct price is 50 rupees. Here take 100." As he gingerly took the note to the approval of his fellow cop-thugs, he began bobbing his head side to side indicating with a pre-planned measure of reluctance that I was free to go, bargain accepted. The other cops on the roadside made a great show of not seeing the monetary exchange. No doubt they will get their share soon ... and in some next life. A receipt would have been out of the question, yet had I insisted one could have doubtlessly been issued from the police station where the outstretched hands of one dozen more brown-uniformed extortionists would be waiting.

An Englishman I once met backpacking in the Himalayas told me of the time that a kindly cop invited him to lunch. The two of them strolled over to a dhaba, a peasant's eatery, and sat down at a table overlooking a spectacular valley. This cop, who appeared cultured and high-ranking, graciously asked the guest what he would like to eat, and then placed his order as well. After lunch and a Thums Up the policeman politely excused himself due to pressing engagements, while the waiter handed the Englishman the bill on cue.

The light is long, very long, and the dust and exhaust fumes choke me. Many of the riders have wrapped up their faces under lengths of gauze-like cotton cloth to keep out the fumes. Slits of dark eyes peering mummy-like from behind cotton masks give the two-wheeling motorists the determined appearance of terrorists on a suicide mission. I look down and check to see that my toes are pointing straight ahead, drawn alongside my bike. Space is at a premium here where three lanes have magically split into eight or nine. Underpaid and under-tested bus drivers from remote villages demonstrate a might-is-right complex by jockeying up next to the two-wheelers and then slowly rolling their huge tires close enough so that the rubber's heat is felt emanating in waves. And neither being a foreigner assures me any protection. Having a sunburned and smiling pink face is fine while you walk through the bazaars and the merchants want to woo your rupees from your wallet with flattery and the offer of a Thums Up. But once you sit upon a bike you have joined India's swirling, rushing whirlpool of well-tanned humanity, and survival becomes the name of the challenge. On these roads survival means stepping down from the royal tourist's throne as you climb into the saddle of a motorcycle, for India's roads have no room for the poser.

The amazing thing is the huge number of near misses that you witness—or almost take part in—per second, here upon the world's most dangerous roadways. When something does go horribly wrong and an accident occurs, a mob will quickly form. In short order the supposed guilty driver is summarily ferreted out and unceremoniously beaten to death. This is not hearsay: I actually witnessed this once while riding through Agra. Hearing an "explosion" like the popping of a huge grape, I glanced over my shoulder to see in horror that a small boy had just stuck his head under the huge, slow-rolling wheel of a bus. Immediately as splattered brains shooting in all directions fell to earth, a swarm of angry men descended upon the rolling megalith. As I threw back the throttle, I could see in my rear-view mirror the loudly protesting driver going down at the 1,000 hands and 10,000 fingers of a wild gang of no less than 500 cursing, screaming men. I did not wait around to witness the driver's fate in the center of that vicious wolf pack. On three other times I have narrowly escaped the savagery of an Indian mob when peaceful, friendly, even kind, men go berserk at the drop of a hat like milk boiling over. After an Indian riot, a night out with the boys, nameless dead, lives utterly wasted, are picked up by burning ground chandalas as the mob, its blood lust satiated, wends its way home for dinner with the family. If, however, the offending driver escapes the mob, then they are just as likely to turn upon the next witless victim who happens to drive their way.

Perhaps citizenry discontent would be better aimed at a city hall that carelessly builds unplanned roads and then neglects their maintenance. Or directed at the state government which hands out licenses to drive without adequate testing or education. Whereas the challenge of riding India's deserts, hills, mountains or jungles is exhilarating and uplifting, biking her city streets even at a stoplight, is a battle for the very right to live.

A woman in her twenties walks through the moving traffic on my left holding the hand of a small child, and crosses casually without looking either way. Apparently she is coming from her astrologer who for ten rupees has informed her, "You will have long life." On the average, nearly four hundred are slaughtered on the streets of Nagpur each year.

Here straddling my Yezdi, the light is painfully long, so I spend a moment sizing up individual faces of the particular crowd I'm standing with. Perhaps there is a "destined crossing" at this particular juncture of time and place, one of those eternal friends you just bump into and feel like you've always known each other. India is the best place to meet such people, due to the average Indian's acceptance of the fact that we are all part and parcel of the same spiritual whole. What is called deja vu in the West is here called *jata-smara*, memory of a past life. Here the explanation why some people become bound as instant friends is a simple one; they were friends in some forgotten previous scenario.

Once in Madras I turned around to find a *dhoti*-clad *brahman*, his forehead neatly marked with tilak, his shikha tuft of hair well tied, smiling upon me.

When I smiled back, my "new, eternal friend," whom I was to know for less than a minute yet will remember for the rest of my life, simply said, "Do you know that feeling of sudden joy that you get, filling you up from within? It means that someplace, someone dear is emanating fond thoughts of you." He went on his way, but doubtless we'll meet for another second in some future birth, at least if I do not achieve the all-transcendent goal of *yoga*. For he who achieves the goal of *yoga* no longer has any use for this world with its temporary affections of society, friendship and love.

On another occasion thirty years ago, a tall-dignified Musalman, strolled up to me as I was purchasing a pair of Kohlapuri sandals at Kalbadevi. He reached down and gently seized the second toe of my right foot and noted that its length exceeds that of my big toe. He casually said, " This shows that you are on a spiritual mission and will succeed in your search through India." Sometimes obscure and ordinary-looking strangers speak with the eternal voice of prophets here in the mystic East.

All around me are dozens of sinewy laborers pulling ancient wooden carts, or lightning-eyed college girls on their way to class delicately perched upon bright step-throughs like the 50cc Luna or 100cc Scooty. In front of me there is a balding husband, his coconut-oiled brown dome baking in the morning sun. Four members of his immediate family are balanced with him upon his 175cc Bajaj, India's incarnation of the Vespa. Here and there are tinny stick shift econo-boxes that only the most frugal American would drive, yet in this land many are navigated by full-time chauffeurs. There are Indian jeeps and vans all stuffed to bursting with three or four generations of over-population. Additionally there must be fifty restless Indian-built, 150cc Indo-Japanese motorcycles piloted by ambitious young men on Indian standard time off to a late start for work. Yet I am alone in a vast crowd today, an isolated twig in a tsunami wave of mankind. Ambition, anxiety and the desire to succeed in a modern world whose tenebrous goals are nowhere understood ensnare each of my temporary neighbors here at the light, as they charge blindfolded into the twenty-first century. At this particular crossroads at least, the rare and serendipitous jewel of an eternal friend is not found.

On my right is a three-wheeler, a scooter ricksha, which has a condom ad pasted on its rear, a taboo subject just twenty-five years ago. In the ad a model smiles temptingly from behind a gigantic rubber. It strikes me that this pretty young hopeful has already torpedoed her career by allowing herself to be typecast. In a rigidly structured society like India's, overcoming the stigma of "condom girl" will be no easy task. I imagine that the ad's Hindi motto says something like, "If Dad had used one of these I wouldn't be here."

As the burning morning sunlight filters through the smog and din, heightening the chiseled features of austere brown faces, I note a bleak seriousness engraved onto each countenance. How true it is that traveling upon the treacherous, rocky, dusty boulevards of the man-made urban hells of India is never the same as negotiating her country roads. There, contemplative brows reflect a more submissive obedience to the Eternal Will personified. In India's countryside, on her fields, around her villages and upon hidden dirt paths, everyone you meet is a *yogi* of some sort.

Whether child or old man, it does not matter, India's rural folk radiate a sort of transcendental happiness. Only a half hour or less from this stoplight, the temporary business of eating, sleeping and procreating is secondary to the duty of preparing for that anticipated ride upon the eternal road. Here in Nagpur, as in any other metropolis, life has decades ago been turned 180 degrees on its head. In the cities spiritual fulfillment is just too distant to reflect upon: to keep the belly full a modern city dweller in India must toil for twelve full hours daily, and slog through this traffic for another two. This is progress; the gift of municipal perdition whose abysmal rush on all sides of me has been unremittingly barricaded by this cursed light.

I reflect back to the first Indian two-wheeled vehicle—a Vespa—that I rode for any appreciable distance here. One day there at a tea stand in Jabalpur, a young gentleman approached me to inquire about my activities in his country. As we spoke, mentioning that I wanted to learn about the local holy spots or the *punya-bhumis*, his interest piqued: "My name is Ram and I am a *brahman*. I will guide you." Out of the crowd had emerged an eternal friend. In fact Ram Mishra became one of this lifetime's best friends ever. Together we'd scooter about to places where gods played in previous *yuga*s, along the ghats of the sacred Narmada, hiking up to temples hidden behind colossal boulders in the hills. We visited *ashrams* where *yogis* perform miracle cures, sat and meditated with pious Hindus who had never before come into face to face contact with Western society.

Once upon the city's narrow lanes, my eyes filled with horror as a huge truck was bearing down upon us. Probably less than a second from under the wheels, I yanked the handlebars obliquely to one side, a left face that doubtless saved our lives. I remember once seeing a picture from the Indian epic *Mahabharata* in which the fierce son of Bhima, Ghatotkacha, by the powers of his *rakshasi* mother, would grow to a huge size each sundown, uprooting helpless warriors upon the Battlefield of Kurukshetra. That's how I felt before the unforgiving, snorting truck, that base iron chariot of Kali Yuga, that day with Ram. Why had this happened? Why were we not killed? How is it that we had been saved?

Five astride a motorcycle: A dozen perish daily on the roads of Nagpur.

Was it I that turned the handlebars, or was some unseen Force looking out for us? Had we escaped a destined moment, or more precisely, had our destined moment not yet arrived? Plainly, for a second, the great, cold hand of death had suddenly appeared to snatch us away, but just as suddenly had withdrawn into the clouds as if the god of death Yamaraja had changed his mind directed by an even higher Authority. In this world death reigns always supreme, but apparently even Yama must obey Higher Commands. Without much thought, we immediately returned to our mission of searching for holy places that day. Minutes later the incident was forgotten, as we found ourselves lost in the serenity of village byways.

About two weeks later, Ram's parents suddenly arranged his marriage. It was not done in the usual festive fashion, but rather like some big secret coming to light. Tongues of bewildered neighbors must have wagged at the suddenness of the event. Not long after the embers of the ghee-soaked fire of the marriage *yagna* had turned cold, it was discovered that the bride was not as youthful as her falsified and ill-matched horoscope had shown. Her parents had made a hurried arrangement to offload a daughter with health problems. The bride was no longer young; she was now approaching middle age. "Although without flames, an unmarried daughter burns the Hindu father like fire," it is said, and the marriage to Ram had been an easy solution.

Ram, too, had had a checkered past, rumors had it, due to the vagaries of youth. On the day that I had met him, I had noticed some of his friends were rough types. But he was a *brahman* with a good heart and by showing me around the *punya-bhumis* of his native Jabalpur, it occurred to me, he was trying to rectify past youthful mischief. Now the misery of Ram's bride was boundless. She had been forced upon her younger husband as much as he had been forced upon her. Due to her chronic female problems, she could not render the service to her husband every Hindu wife would love to give.

A few days after the marriage, she went into the bathroom, doused herself with kerosene, and lit herself on fire. Ram tried valiantly to put the flames out with the very arms that could not embrace her, but he instead became consumed by the holocaust. The couple, who could not live as one here, left this world as one in a pyre.

A week or so on, Ram's father came to me and we solaced one another as confused and blind mortals try to do. He knew that I had studied the Vedic astrology of the Hindus, and he brought Ram's horoscope with him. Mostly I couldn't look at the stars that day, which requires an impersonal detachment, so we spent some hours talking of the vagaries of life, destiny and most of all my personal affection for his gentle son Ram. I recalled how he had guided me to so many hidden places like Siddheshwar Cave, Shani Tirtha, Gupteshwara, and Gwari Ghat. I still enjoy visiting these places today. And in a way Ram is still with me when I do. I still see his father, who never recovered from the tragedy, Hindus having no pretense to the politically correct pretension of "closure" as we have in the West.

Despite the poisonous exhaust fumes, the taciturn cops, the blazing sun, the bus trying to roll over my toes, or my grim memories, the thought somehow never leaves me that somehow I am lucky to be here. True, I've met my share of cursing and complaining foreigners who cannot wait to fly out of India, who worship the jetliner as a saving god from the sky that will carry them back to the predictable security of America or Europe. I once heard of a traveler who landed at Calcutta, and caught a taxicab that got lost in Bengal's torrential overflow of humanity. After a few hours of ensnarled third world traffic he had had enough. The traveler's pioneer spirit bruised, the would-be explorer ordered the driver back to the airport where he caught the next plane out of the City of the Black Hole.

I knew a fellow American here who after a month in the exotic East had had enough. Blubbering like a baby, he climbed a tall building in Bombay and threatened to jump–unless a representative of his embassy, Big Brother with a Ticket, would come to fly him back home to the States. It is true that while some travelers go crazy in India, others say that they were crazy to come here in the first place. But for the determined wanderer with the single-minded concentration to pierce through the curtain that hides Vedic India, suddenly that which is most ancient appears sane. And that which was left behind in the fast-food and toilet paper civilization becomes insane.

Perhaps one of the problems with Indians, at least the ones I see here at this infernal stoplight, is that they have developed no appreciation for the richness of their venerable heritage. They are waging all their stakes upon a future of vacuous promises in exchange for a rich culture older than any other on Earth. Of course this is quite understandable after the imposition of more than 1,000 years of foreign rule, beginning with the Afghan Mahmud Ghazni. Even the word Hindu is a foreign term, given to them by invaders who could not correctly pronounce Sindhu, the sixth of the holy rivers. There is a joke amongst religious scholars that goes, "The word Hindu is nowhere in the Hindu scriptures."

The ancient name of this land is Bharat and the religion is *sanatana dharma*, "eternal service to God." Whether the Persians, the Dutch, the French, the Portuguese, the British, the Christian missionaries, or powerful "friends" like the Russians, the modus operandi of the colonialist and religious missionary has been to impress upon the Indian the inferiority of the richest and longest-lived culture on earth. With their sacred cow milked dry and readied for slaughter by imported steel blades, demoralized generations became apologetic and even ashamed of their birthright and religion.

To rationalize themselves and their heritage, Indian intellectual apologists began to compare the salient features of their vast sub-continent with acceptable foreign places they were taught to admire. Kashmir became the Switzerland of India. Poona, or now Pune, became the Oxford and Cambridge of India. Lord Krishna's birthplace at Mathura has been compared to Jerusalem, though Krishna appeared thousands of years before Jesus. The great historical epics the

Ramayana and *Mahabharata* became the (much more recent) Iliad and Odyssey of India. Indians have even claimed that the dasha *avataras*, Hinduism's ten incarnations of God, represent a sort of early tribal understanding of Darwinian evolution. Bombay, where more invidious films are made than any place on earth, has become Bollywood, to the chagrin of the aging traditionalists who, longing for the rebirth of the more sober Vedic Age, point to many current Hindu revivalist movements. As I survey this town through hot dust and exhaust fumes, it occurs to me that nobody has ever had the temerity to compare Nagpur to anywhere else.

Here on India's roadways, in her villages, towns and cities, in her forests and jungles, I am often reminded of the poem about the six blind men of old Hindustan who tried to describe an elephant to each other. The one who grabbed the tail thought the elephant to be like a rope, the one who latched onto the trunk, thought it resembled a snake, and so on. For one traveler India is an adventurer-rich paradise; and for another it is a dishonest, crazy, diseased and poverty-stricken hellhole. For one it is a journey into new regions of thought, philosophy and enlightenment. For the next India is a trip back in time to the Dark Ages. For me, who has derived so much from this gentle, brutal land; it is impossible to look without condescension upon those foreign travelers who come here expecting the homage that their greenbacks certainly bring at some tourist resort. True, the amateur tourist unceremoniously discarded from India like a reject from boot camp deserves pity as doubtless many foreigners pity me just for liking it here. From my point of view, the travelers who succeed and thrive here comprise the highest echelon of world wayfarer. They are not your Club Med, planned vacation types. The proper wayfarer or pilgrim here is like Mark Twain who wrote, "India is the land that all men long to see, and having seen by so much as a glimpse, would not trade that glimpse for all the other sights of the world. This land has an irresistible appeal to alien prince and alien peasant alike." Lowell Thomas, another great American adventurer, wrote, "(India), I realized, was by far the most fascinating of all the countries I had visited...when I saw India I knew that I was witnessing the greatest show of all. I had found Australia and New Zealand fascinating, Africa full of thrills and surprises, and the Far East absorbingly interesting. But India towers as far above them as the Himalayas tower above the Alps. As a spectacle, there is nothing like it. Variety, we are assured, is the spice of life. The country that interests us the most is the one where there is the most variety...And India has variety to the nth degree. It is supremely the land of the startling contrast. The southern tip touches the equator. Central India is in the Temperate Zone and is not only a land of mighty rivers and fertile valleys, but also includes vast deserts similar to those of Arabia, Arizona and the Sahara. Along the northern border of India loom those towering mountain ranges, the Himalayas, loftiest of all the peaks of earth, their summits clad with ice and snow since the dawn of time...Who holds India, holds the world. As a theory of world-politics you can pick it to pieces, but you cannot escape its seductive glamorous persuasion ... India is a land of splendor and magnificence far, far surpassing anything to be found in either Europe or America—and at the same time it is also a land of squalor and misery so terrible that the mere mention of it makes me shudder. I had thought of India as a country one could see, and be satisfied to come away from, in a month or two. But instead of two months, I stayed for two years. Even then I was not content. I wanted to stay on and on."

Lowell Thomas continues: "Every traveler from the West who visits India should have a *guru*, a wise man, to lead him about and explain the strange things he sees and hears. Without a *guru* the European or American who sojourns for a little while in India wanders as in a daze and comes away as bewildered as any Alice in Wonderland. But to find your *guru* when you get to India, ah, that may not be so easy." Considering that these words were written in 1929 before the rush of Western *yogis* to the mystic East, they are strikingly profound.

Yet even for the successful tourist, the spiritual pilgrim, there is another sort of pitfall. Like crocodiles in the Ganges or serpents in the sandal tree, there are many "business *gurus*," ordinary, unqualified men who enjoy posing as extraordinary spiritual masters just to make a cheap living off foolish disciples. The simple formula they employ to accomplish this act of cheating their victims is usually based around a standard formula of verbal legerdemain. Bob Dylan did not mince words when he summed up this formula as "kill them with self-confidence, while poisoning them with words." Usually, the slick pretender *swami* begins with something like: "Yes, yes! You are God. But now you have forgotten your supreme divinity. I shall make you God again. Give me some money."

Although there are literally thousands of such saffron-clad flimflam men sermonizing carbon copies of the same humbug, duped followers become so hypnotized that they remain loyal only to their particular charlatan. In reality, the *shastras* of India teach that truth can be found in many places without compromising unflinching dedication to one true master. In fact it is a common test for the worthy disciple to remain staunch in his vows before the temptations of the world. If any and all of the business *gurus* are the same Supreme God, and the message of becoming God is one, then it should make little difference which one is consulted. The naïve students explain: "I am not *there* yet. Everyone is

God, but for now only my *guru* is God." Or could it be that he just needs the money more than some other god?

Bewildered disciples of *yogadom's* con artists are easily recognized by their blissful glow, their smug and all-knowing conversation and theatrical walk. The more money they have been cheated out of, the more exaggerated their histrionics. Many have neo-Sanskrit names, which they themselves find unpronounceable. It is quite natural in life that the more one has been cheated, like falling under some fortune-teller's scam, the less likely one is to admit it, at least until abject bankruptcy forces the issue. The more money that is "donated" to line this or that *bhogi yogi's* pocket, the more the disciple becomes *yogafied* in feel-good self-promotion to a staged trance. Insecurities of the poser *guru* are revealed by the fact that he fences his disciples like barnyard animals within the *ashram* walls. Sometimes, even this is not enough. Recently when one so-called god-man of India was accused of child molestation, the "master" ordered his disciples to observe vows of silence and to avoid the internet at the risk of excommunication. For some strange reason no such restrictions were in place before the scandal broke, as long as he could hear the singing of his glories from all corners.

At India's great religious fairs like the Kumbha Mela or Magha Mela, it is possible to have the darshan of many genuine spiritualists who practice various forms of *yoga*: *karma*, *hatha*, *ashtanga*, or *bhakti*. However understanding these true ascetics and the land, Mother India, that has given them birth, requires a radical mental adjustment for most Westerners. My own Guru Maharaja, while surveying the vast congregation of *yogis* at the Kumbha Mela, observed that the vast majority was genuine. The problem for the Western seeker is that he will likely become attracted to the imitation *yogis* who canvass him with flattering words and wise-sounding quips about "becoming God."

Once while traveling through the Khyber Pass on a bus, I noticed that a French couple in the seat in front of me had just discovered the loss of their gold pen. They were animatedly discussing each poor person they'd met, and which one could likely have stolen it. I leaned forward, "Did you meet anyone else?" "Yes, just one other young gentleman. But it couldn't have been him. He was rich and his father owned a bank." So I replied, "Then he is the culprit who stole your pen." It is often quite impossible to determine who is the actual poor man in South Asia. Generally, they who are well to do never boast. "Your smooth-talking acquaintance was probably a skilled con artist who targets innocent tourists." The way of the imitation *guru* is no different.

The truth is that invariably many posers will step forward just to cheat the innocent aspirant. What they usually have in common is an oversimplified method of instant nirvana combined with an urgent need for money. *Yoga* for suckers. One such bogus *guru* told his disciples that the lamb is the symbol of Christ, it goes baa baa, and since he is called *Baba*, he is the Christ incarnate.

It is a mistake therefore to assume that, once having decided to adopt a spiritual path, one will automatically be safe and protected. He who carelessly dives in headfirst may find shallow waters. A few years down the road, abused and dejected spiritual dropouts are found reciting the usual pitiable *ashram* horror stories. The exact offenses of imposter *swamis* and holy mothers are too innumerable to recount. Many of their ridiculous antics in the theater of playing God would be funny, except for the human life and dignity that has been trampled upon just to keep one man propped up on his flimsy throne. At the root of it all will invariably be found a pretender's insatiable lust and greed, manifested as a desire for sex, money and power over less aggressive souls. Unfortunately, it is generally almost impossible to help others who will pay money to be lied to and flattered. At the end of the day, the one who wants to be cheated will find a suitable cheater.

I can recall a thousand events involving such rascals. Yet the single most egregious assault upon *dharma* that comes to mind whenever I recall swamidom's robed serpents occurred in 1981 or '82 while I was in Lucknow. There was at that time an imposter going by the bogus name of "Pilot *Baba*" attracting a wide following based upon his hollow promises of divinity. This false ascetic latched onto a deaf mute and, robing him in the saffron attire of a *yogi*, ceremoniously lowered him into the ground and buried him. This so-called Pilot *Baba* then announced amidst much festivity that he would unearth the mute some weeks later at which time he would peacefully awaken from his *yoga* trance. The charlatan offered his foolish following a chance to sacrifice their hard-earned money at the burial site, promising that whatever was given would be returned many times over. Word spread quickly and soon a queue of illiterate and greedy Indian followers formed daily throwing whatever rupees they could spare in hopes of future wealth. Eventually a bad smell began to rise from the meditation chamber, which even Pilot *Baba* with his cunning and silver tongue had a hard time explaining away. Soon an angry mob of investors formed, and to their horror found that the deaf mute "*yogi*" was in an advanced stage of decay. Yet the murderous Pilot *Baba* was nowhere to be found; he had absconded with every *rupee*.

I have come across many of the imitation variety of *yogis* over the years, but the most comical was the *baba*–or rather buffoon–of Sai Land. Sai Land was a desolate portion of beach north of Bombay that had been roped off to rope in fools. Not far from where fishermen of mixed Portuguese and Hindu descent cast their nets, the beach was an unlikely site for a *yogi* in meditation. But the Sai Land *yogi* had created an instant *ashram* like a fisherman throws his net. As I was strolling along the shore with a friend, the so-called *baba's* English-speaking cohort approached us with broken syllables and an urgent invitation to meet the Sai Land *baba*. There on the other side of the rope, the empowered *Baba* sat pensively before cold embers. In hushed, confidential tones the henchman communicated to my friend and me that the Sai Land *baba* was such an astute *yogi* he could rope his penis to the bumper of a car, pulling the car by walking backwards. As proof of the *Baba's* mystic abilities, he would condescend to cut an unpeeled banana inside its skin simply by chanting *mantras*.

The *baba* of Sai Land huffed and puffed, tossed some ash from his dead fire over three carefully laid bananas, and whispered a few unintelligible incantations. Then with a somber glance and black finger he sternly ordered me to peel one of the bananas. Lo and behold, the banana inside was indeed cut in three. "So when will the *baba* pull the car with his *lulu*?" I asked the stooge using a colloquial term for the male member. By now I was having difficulty keeping a straight face, but my sarcasm had flown over his greedy head.

"Yes, yes. *Baba* is eager to demonstrate his power of *yoga*," came the equally straight-faced reply. "But it will take one month of rigid *tapasya*. You now give *baba* 200 rupees. Funds he will use for maintaining Sai Land as he readies for strenuous exercise."

By way of replying, I pointed to two pinholes in the bananas' peels by which the two fruits had been earlier cut with a needle through the skin. No longer could I contain myself, and laughing out loud like one who had just enjoyed a good joke, I put down the fruit casually refusing to eat a piece as "prasad." The two hucksters that day were left without even a rupee for their grand show. The *baba's* head was now beginning to swiftly bob side to side, his detached pose now having been replaced by an angry let's-get-back-to-the-drawing-board expression. A few weeks later I chanced to walk up the same wide, palm-lined beach and found no sign of Sai Land. The old fraud must have known that the show must move on. He had pulled up stakes for good and the monsoon high tide had washed away any traces of the imposter.

In the *Ramayana*, when the demon Ravana came to kidnap the Goddess of Fortune Sita, he did so in the saffron attire of an ascetic holy man. Today in every religion in every corner of Earth cheating is a common practice. Even true renunciates have been waylaid by worldly desires.

The quest for the Absolute Truth, inner transcendence and spiritual happiness in God, rises above mundane religion, dogma, mere morality and altruistic service performed for the benefit of other conditioned souls. The ultimate satisfaction of inner illumination, as stated in the 700 verses of *Bhagavad-gita As It Is*, rests in humbling oneself in a mood of surrender before the Supreme Lord in an attitude of service and devotion. The *yoga* of pure love of God is far above ill-considered sectarianism: it is the eternal force and function of the soul who shares in the dedicated quest for service to the One without a second. That *jiva* soul who has achieved an affectionate, personal reciprocation with the spiritual whole, the Supreme Personality of Godhead Krishna, is the true knower of *yoga*. Above the *yoga* of work called *karma*, or the *yoga* of asceticism called *hatha*, or the *yoga* of wisdom called jnana, is the *yoga* of ecstatic devotional love called *bhakti*.

Finding a true, disinterested and transcendental *guru* and guide on the path to *samadhi*, wherein the mind becomes lovingly fixed upon the Lord's service, is the only key to unlocking the gate on the royal road to enlightenment. In China this path is called Tao, "the way" or "the path." Thousands of years ago Chinese monks made the hazardous and arduous trek through the valleys of the Himalayas and came to India, the Motherland of civilization and religion, to study. Over time, this word *dharma*, the spiritual path, became mispronounced in China as tao.

In fact, the concept of *dharma*, loosely translated as "religion." actually explains the original transcendental work of the anti-material being. Just as fire is always hot and ice is always cold, so the awakening of *dharma* is the eternal sustaining nature of the soul now hidden behind the curtain of *maya*. *Dharma* is sometimes confused as one sectarian religion or another, but superficial concepts of religion can never satisfy the quest of the *atma* particle searching for an ultimate union-in-separation with the Spiritual Whole. True *dharma* is *sanatana-dharma*, the eternal religion of ecstatic love of God.

Likewise, the Chinese were aware of the system of *dhyana* or meditation, which they mispronounced as "zen." Hence "Tao of religion" or "Zen meditation" are repetitive phrases. Just as these transcendental concepts had spread north into China from India, so were they carried thousands of years ago to the Near East, to Northern Africa, and on into Europe. The archaeological evidence relating to India's cultural gifts, though profound, has been ignored by scholars who are unwilling to put aside bias. Not only do India's Sanskrit histories, the *Puranas*, give accounts of ancient Vedic civilizations far from what is today known as India, but ruins of old temples in the near East, and the Sanskrit inscription at the fire temple near Baku, Azerbaijan confirm the practice

A sea of humanity frozen for a moment in time…by a red light in Nagpur.

of Hinduism in distant regions. Although Vedic civilization has been narrowed, India's torchlight message of *Bhagavad-gita* lives on, translated in dozens of languages worldwide.

The *Bhagavad-gita* has seen as much abuse as any other scripture of the world in the hands of self-interested men. To give the appearance of piety, politicians even today enjoy waving the *Gita* at rallies. University scholars both in the East as well as in the West seek acceptance by continuing to offer novel self-serving interpretations, which have nothing to do with the *Gita*'s actual message of *mam ekam saranam vraja*: surrender to Godhead. Posers still twist the purport of the *Gita* just to waylay the aspirant into their prehensile grasp. Though truth is everywhere, truth can be difficult to find like light that takes on the color of glass through which it filters. To know India's culture, one must learn the *yoga* of the *Bhagavad-gita As It Is*, and this is no easy task.

There is an allegory about a sea turtle that comes up for air only once each year. Somewhere on the ocean is floating a piece of driftwood with a knot-hole. The allegory asks what are the chances that the turtle's head could poke through the hole in the wood? The answer: exactly the same as a seeker has of meeting a genuine spiritual master, a realized devotee of the Lord. Exactly the same as stumbling upon the Absolute Truth in the forest of delusion.

As mentioned earlier, it is the difference between the way that life's stage play is acted out here in India, and the routine a foreigner calls normal, that can literally cause a Westerner to go mad. All this serves to underscore the would-be

Then the light turns green...

yogi's need for a *guru* and guide. Flip-outs are quite common among wayfarers here who expect their trip to glide along in some predictable routine.

I once saw an American actually go berserk right inside a police station, in front of the commanding officer of a Bombay precinct. While I was having a pleasant chat with the cops, who by then had all become my friends, in walks this scruffy relic of 60's America, protesting everything that, according to his point of view, was wrong with India. Junior officers bristled as they were forced to watch their commanding officer brook a barrage of verbal assaults. Finally the crazed hippie ripped off his shirt and prepared to throw it at the cops. I decided to do what I had seen so many gentle Hindus do in the face of one of their own offensive brethren. I stood up, turned the startled hippie about, marched him out the door, and tossed his shirt in his direction. Then I turned to face the cops, and with my best Hindu manners said, "Please forgive my fellow American for his misdeeds." As my blanket apology was accepted, I reflected that had I had a Hindu mother, she would have been proud of me.

Had I not intervened, the bewildered adventurer would have spent a month in a dungeon-like jail before anyone from his embassy got wind of it. But the point is that without a guide India and its ways are confusing and even flabbergasting to the uninitiated. The great travel-adventure writer Lowell Thomas was grateful for his guide in the 1920's, and half a century later as I straddle my Yezdi at the stoplight in Nagpur I am none the different. Without the grace of

Shri Guru all that I will see in India would appear as mad and ridiculous as the antics of mental patients. But there is a method to the madness of India, a sublime reason for its ways. Appreciating that there is order in the chaos of Mother India requires not only an open mind, but eyes, too, that have been forcibly opened by the torchlight of knowledge. The word 'man' has been derived from the Sanskrit *manasa*, meaning 'mind'. The lucky soul who has achieved the rare human form of birth should live thoughtfully, considering the consequences of mindless sense gratification. It is this ability to think and to reason that separates man from the animals. Perfection of reasoning and intelligence is found in the achievement of *yoga*. *Yoga* does not mean a mindless twisting of the body or elaborate enjoyment of sex, a so-called pleasure which is freely available to dogs and cats."

And so it is that I have usually been able to feel fortunate while traveling in India, but here I must emphasize "usually." For even the toughest, shrewdest and most savvy travelers, India can be a very daunting challenge at best. Forget about trying to solve the myriad of India's problems; just by coming here you are going to invariably find a new set of your own problems that you never knew existed. Fledgling travelers are quickly separated from the pros in short order. Enlightenment, spiritual elevation and *samadhi* come with a stiff price tag. Tolerance is the key. When nagging problems arise—or even if disaster strikes—the lone wayfarer must repeat to himself *mantra*-like, "This is all happening to me due to my own *karma*. Had I not caused difficulties to other living entities in my past life, then today I would not be suffering the reactions to my transgressions. My own arrogance is the root of my own pain. I will pray to God, to Bhagavan or 'He who is supreme', to protect me. I will try to be humble in the future." Nonetheless, it is better for beginners here to travel first class, to stay in proper hotels, to associate exclusively with the cultured and educated, and as a general rule to avoid diving headfirst into murky waters. If and when you get your wheels in India, go practice riding on the left side of the road on some out-of-the-way country lane. For the motorcyclist, India is the speed freak's nightmare and the lane-splitter's paradise. In the final analysis, India is a very, very dangerous place, a razor's edge from which you can easily slip and crash at any moment.

Extensive travel in India has left me with a bulging portfolio of horror stories. I usually do not discuss them simply because they will not be believed in the coddled and nourished West. Here in the land I have somehow grown to love I have been at the center of three major riots and have been held prisoner against my will thrice. I'll never forget the first time that I saw a dead man lying on the road, flies all over him, waiting patiently for the chandalas to come and cremate him. People walked by pretending not to notice. In Ayodhya, I once had a refreshing dip in an inviting pond, and seeing a friendly stranger beside a fire on the shore, swam to that side to warm myself. I then spotted a lean brown leg protruding from the fire, and I was unwittingly attending a funeral. No mourners were present. Having died alone in this world, this Hindu man had nonetheless died gloriously, for he had left this world from the city of the birth of Lord Rama. I once toured the birthplace of Lord Krishna, Mathura, with a God-brother who left the next day for Jaipur six hours south to visit the Govindaji Mandir there. On the way his bus crashed, and my friend from that point on began the rest of his young life in a wheel chair, paralyzed from the waist down.

In this wonderful, horrible country, I have been robbed, hijacked, pick-pocketed, and have suffered many a serious illness. I was in an accident in Madras where I was treated by a quack doctor with sugar pills for a week while I was hemorrhaging, an injury that later had to surgically corrected at Jaslok Hospital in Bombay by the able hands of Dr. Thakurlal Motwani.

Once with my brother in *yoga*, Vaikunthanath, I decided to jump into the flooded Yamuna River at Vrindavan and let the current carry us the ten miles downstream to Mathura. We were wearing *gumchas*, small waist cloths, and the plan was to get a cycle ricksha at the other end. The river was very deep; we were excited to be swimming over the tops of trees, yet the current was not treacherous. At times villagers would notice two foreigners dog paddling in a place we should not have been. They would come out and shout warnings to us in Hindi. I thought they were cautioning us about the current, but we found out later that what they were saying was this: "Cobras have been washed from their holes, they are quite perturbed, and you are swimming with them!"

In Bombay I once witnessed a man beaten to death within arm's length. He died with a silly half-grin on his face, falling like a felled tree, his head bouncing upon the cold concrete like a rubber ball. It would have been comical and cartoon-like, if it were not for the stark reality of life's last curtain call played out before me with all its finality. When I was asked by the police to narrate my version of the events as a witness, I was instead accused of the crime ... for every Indian knows that all white men are filthy rich and will lavishly bribe everyone in sight. I hardly had two rupees to rub together, so I languished for some weeks in a horrible jail with several others accused along with me, and spent the next year on trial for murder. Can you believe that in this Bombay jail, this so-called "lock-up," 120 men lived in four small cells? There was water for only one hour daily, and the only toilet was a hole in the floor. By midday a 24-inch fetid mound of fecal matter had arisen above the hole. Yet the worse part was that to get to the "toilet," you had to wade through a 6-foot wide 3-inch deep puddle of urine. No, there was no exercise room, legal library or television. When ordinary citizens didn't have these things, why should prisoners? If many Indians must go without water, then certainly prisoners should, too, guilty or not. In America if a pet is treated the way Indian prisoners are treated, then the owner himself would be jailed, with a clean cell with his own toilet.

At the murder trial, six foreigners and two Indians stood accused. I remember seeing the prosecutor producing blood-soaked garments of the many "victims." "Where did those come from," I asked. "They are soaked in chicken blood," our lawyer explained. "It is a very common practice." At one point in the trial, an agitated witness pointed at me, accusing me in Marathi. Later I was narrated a translation of the "testimony." The witness had said under oath that I had beaten him on the back with a stick pointing to the chicken blood that was spilled all over the back of the shirt. My lawyer then asked him, "Since you were being beaten on the back, then how can you identify who struck you?" Eventually a not guilty verdict was returned as far as "the Bombay Six" were concerned. One Indian named Adhikary was found guilty of the murder, and in proper Indian legal fashion, it was the wrong man. Within a few weeks, I was on my way out of India to Bangkok.

I had met a cargo pilot during my trial who had been fired as a passenger pilot back in America due to his age. He now flew a DC–3 full of goats from India to Arabia, and offered to fly me out of India to escape a murder conviction. Had I accepted, and it was tempting, then the other five non-Indians on trial with me would have all been rounded up and immediately imprisoned. So I put my faith in God and stayed. This pilot told me that "the world ends at Istanbul and begins again at Bangkok." I was in the middle of a No Man's Land on trial for murder, yet after a year was found not guilty.

I remember that once a State government wanted to change the name of a college and the ensuing riot over the issue killed hundreds. Perhaps most of the dead had never been to college. But this is how riots can happen in this country and the wary visitor must understand this.

The worst riot I ever "attended" was in one of the world's most overpopulated places, at the most crowded place and time. It was Calcutta's Sealdah Station at rush hour. Apparently some of my fellow passengers did not like me for a riot erupted. I ran out of the station and jumped into a taxi, which the crowd of hundreds proceeded to destroy in short order. I decided to confront the mob so

I exited the taxi, the windows of which had by this time been smashed. Just a few days earlier, I had read an account of how Gandhi had quelled a mob simply by chanting the name of "Rama." I likewise tried this technique, screaming "Rama" repeatedly at the top of my voice, and succeeded only in infuriating the mob all the more. Things had changed in the thirty-five years from the time of Gandhi till 1982.

At the time of the riot, Indian cars still had a long steel device with which to manually crank over the engine in case of a dead battery, like old Model T's. The trunk was opened and this rod was taken from the trunk to be used as a club to beat me to death. Eventually I was stripped bare naked, before a crowd of thousands. This went on for forty-five minutes until the police showed up. The police formed a "lathi-charge," which is a method of weighing into a crowd with long wooden sticks called lathis. Hundreds of chappels, or leather sandals, were left on the street as hundreds of barefoot cowards ran home to their mothers. Bengal, home of Calcutta, is the most extreme place in a land of extremes. Some of the world's greatest writers, *yogis* and philosophers have been Bengalis.

Although I am more cautious now in my view of India, I have been drawn back here time and again over the years, although I have no plans ever to return to Calcutta. What is the mystical lure of India? Why does the lotus grow in mud? I know first hand that this country can be cruel and rough, terribly rough. But I am neither complaining nor bragging. Complaining would mean that the humble message of *mea culpa* would not have been learned. Bragging would invite more unwelcome visitations of past bad *karma*. Yet anything worth having is worth the fight and the wounds. Is this not the message of *Bhagavad-gita*? There upon the Battlefield of Kurukshetra, Shri Krishna did not instruct His warrior-disciple Prince Arjuna to become a monk and retire to a mountain cave. The Lord ordered, "Fight the good battle, Arjuna, and win the good fight. Do your duty and do not be a coward. Unmanliness does not become a *kshatriya*."

Would-be Western *yogis* who are unhappy in India do have my sympathy–many would be better suited to a packaged adventure in Disneyland, which is what most *swami's* offer anyway. In India if something goes wrong, you are at the mercy of your fate: you do not consult an attorney or insurance agent, you consult your *karma*. Still, for me at least, the good experiences have edged out the bad ones. The real *yogis*, whom it has been my rare privilege to meet, the Vedic scholars who have instructed me, the tens of thousands of holy places and temples unto which I have bowed, the sacred lore that has opened up its mysterious yet universal truths to me, and everywhere the brown-eyed children that have called me "uncle": all these have all made India a wonderful and memorable ride. Neither is there anything in this world for which I would trade my India experience. My regret is that I do not have enough years in this body to relish the divine truths of this land and its ways over and over again.

Besides, living in America and Europe is not always easy either, though technology is ever working to make it as humdrum as possible. The old book of wise tales *Hitopadesh* of Narayana relates the story of a bald man whose scalp was baked by the sun. He escaped to the shelter and shade of a coconut tree, wherefrom at that moment a coconut dropped. Impelled by destiny it landed upon the man's head. *Karma* will visit the doer for better or worse sooner or later, no matter where he tries to hide. Pointing an accusing finger at India for her supposed affronts to me would only point three fingers at myself. Pausing for a moment, I would remember such times as when I have seen people shot while seated next to me in North Carolina, or have died in front of me of stab wounds in San Francisco. Or of the several times I have been attacked and beaten in New York, or robbed in California. The near shipwreck on the English Channel, or the 7.1 San Francisco earthquake I survived. The suicides I have chanced to witness on American bridges, or the headless corpse of my friend who seconds before was resting beside me in the speeding van. How is it that when these things happen in India, we blame it on a third world lack of development, and when they happen back home we close our eyes and pretend that we will be still somehow be protected by fallible science, our bipartisan government and top heavy health plans?

Karma will follow the doer to any part of the world, or material universe, or even into outer space. That place where we can hide from the reactions to our past transgressions over the rights of other living entities has yet to be created. Each of our acts is engraved into the akashic record to be read by the King of Death, Yama, at some future date. Like seeds that will fructify in due time, that which we have done today has indelibly created our future. Temporary enjoyment or suffering, happiness and distress, all these are results of that which we have done before. Noting the temporal state of joy and sorrow, the true *yogi* eschews both and prays only to sip the nectar of eternal knowledge. The middle road of detached renunciation is the transcendental way to the eternal world hidden beyond all reactions to our transgressions. Whenever I see the dhobi washermen pounding white dhotis upon the river's shore, I am reminded that layers of my sins buried for lifetimes are getting pummeled out like dirt from white cloth, often uncomfortably so, with every penitent step, or every turn of the throttle, here in the ancient land of India.

It's amazing what thoughts can roll through your head at an Indian stoplight. During the reign of Mataji, the formidable Indira Gandhi, India manufactured only two cars, the Padmini and the Ambassador. The Padmini was–and is–an Indian Fiat. The Ambassador, the preferred vehicle for government officials, is a 1958 Morris Oxford still made to this day. Like the borrowed motorcycle designs of the Czech Jawa or the British Royal Enfield, these cars have been neatly Xeroxed.

But with the booming silicon chip based economy of the 1980's, many Indians became relatively rich by heading to America. By that time Indira Gandhi had been gunned down at her Delhi home by her disgruntled Sikh bodyguards. By that time, too, her son Sanjay, who had been groomed for the post of Prime Minister, had died while piloting his private plane. To fill the dynastic void, Indira's younger son Rajiv gave up his career as a commercial pilot and was called upon to enter politics. The grandson of Jawaharlal Nehru, son of a Parsi or Zoroastrian father and Hindu *brahman* mother, married a Cambridge-educated Catholic beauty from Italy. Before Rajiv followed his mother to martyrdom, this time by Tamil separatists from Shri Lanka, the new India of foreign goods and cars he created, combined with a flow of silicon-based American dollars, created a formula for crowded highways. Families that once could barely afford a scooter now motored about in chauffeured cars. The problem was, the home government had failed to keep up and there just were not any real highways for all the new cars. Except around Delhi, where Rajiv and his family had lived, India had no decent roads to speak of.

By the 21st century, cars upon India's roadways included domestically built Fords, Hyundais, Mitsubishis, Suzukis, Daiwoos, and even Mercedes. Truck and van companies like Tata, Fairdeal, and Hindustan were now manufacturing roomy utilitarian wagons and sedans. Yet despite the tax-base advantage the government has received from the sale and import of so many cars and trucks, relatively little has been spent on either roadway improvement or driver education. Neither has the issue of passenger protection been given much thought by politicians whose only real job is to hold onto power.

Just as in the old days when overloaded bullocks were worked to death despite Jain posters in the marketplace warning farmers of sorrowful next life retribution, so today trucks and buses are heaped with goods and human cargo until their suspension systems simply give out. Encumbered behemoths carelessly wobble down worn-out roadways at terrific speeds, leaning obliquely to one side because of broken springs and dead shocks. Buses with welded iron bars that block windows jail-cell-like roll off bridges, regularly drowning fifty or sixty at a time. Mothers walking their toddlers meander in and out of traffic as though

AFTERWORD

Yoga Is

SAGES, HAVING FOUND THE HIGHEST PINNACLE of transcendence, teach that every activity of our lives should be directed towards achieving *yoga;* whether breathing, eating, working, raising a family or taking the daily ride on the motorcycle. There is only one *yoga,* and that is the one that helps us to find our harmony with Nature, to move with the heartbeat of Nature, all the while transcending Nature. Many points are crossed in the great climb towards *yoga,* yet the goal of the practice is one.

The true *yogi* aspires neither to make the Sun rise nor set: he is more concerned with the mastery of his senses than mastering the Universe. He adores alone the Supreme Person whose inconceivable energies are the creative force behind all harmony of the cyclic worlds. He who understands that the strings of illusion that control us, must be exchanged for those strings that are manipulated by the Supreme Puppeteer, alone knows *yoga.* Yet the knowledge of higher realms must come with a stiff price tag. In the quest for *yoga* many aspirants have rightly sacrificed transitory pleasures in search of liberation in the Supreme Absolute Truth. Only he who dwells in a fool's paradise can expect to go to sleep on the lap of illusion and awaken in the arms of God. Since God consciousness cannot be purchased in the market place, all that we have to offer to the Yogeshwar is our loving service, *bhakti-yoga,* in reciprocation with His supreme love. Neither are any of our worldly possessions of any value to the Supreme *Yogi.*

India, the land of *yoga,* lies hidden behind a curtain of stray dogs and hungry pigs. Leave aside that these creatures are also souls in transition, conditioned entities confined by deeds of past lives. The pious man consciously or unconsciously treads a thousand steps upon the path of *yoga* in the course of a single day. In the world of *yoga*, very often the true *yogi* is impossible to see.

Although the goal of *yoga* is one, and the consciousness of the fixed mind to achieve *yoga* is one, the passage is fluid and flexible. Since each one of us is an individual, each path must be unique. The Yogeshswar knows this, for there could be no individuality in souls without their having been reflected from the Supreme Individual. For me, *yoga* is a motorcycle ride into *samadhi*, the fixed mind trance of the mystics. When I ride my motorcycle I see the bliss that is *yoga* all around me, in the form of the sky, the wind, the breath that nourishes my soul, and the Hands that control whatever is in Nature. In fact...

Yoga is that force which is communicated like some very subtle electricity through the wire of initiation by the bona fide *guru*.

Yoga is achievable only in this human form of existence.

Yoga is the only means to know the Yogeshwar.

Yoga is performing every deed and activity for the satisfaction of the spirit.

Yoga is that force that links the fragmented infinitesimal spirit soul with the Supreme Spirit Whole.

Yoga is the knowledge that you are consciousness, or rather that your consciousness is the symptom of the *atma*—your very self.

Yoga is an agreement to accept the shelter of He who shelters the Universe.

Yoga is an awakening of the inner principle, a slow and steady movement towards transcendence.

Yoga is knowing your place in the cosmos and beyond the cosmos.

Yoga is the transcendence of *maha-maya* to dwell in *yogamaya*.

Yoga is vertical, whereas illusion is horizontal.

Yoga is getting on your own two wheels because it forces you to get away from all the craziness that you have called normal in this world, to confront your own self by your own inner balance, in some new place where you've never been before.

Yoga is finding the answers to the questions: Who am I? Where have I come from? Where am I going?

Yoga is the ride of a lifetime, the ride into infinity.

Yoga is that which Arjuna found in the ride in the chariot driven by Krishna.

Om Tat Sat

THE AUTHOR

Addressing the crowd of Sofia Rathayatra, 2018

Patita Pavana Dasa Adhikary was born in 1947 in Los Angeles on the night of Rukmini Dwadashi, during Vaishakha Shukla. Later, by Shrila Prabhupada's grace, the city became known as New Dwaraka to the devotees, and the home of Shri Rukmini-Dwarakadisha.

After high school, in 1966, Patita left his then home in Huntington, Long Island, and journeyed to California in search of a guru. After experiencing the counterculture of Haight-Ashbury, he found his spiritual path in 1967 when he encountered the followers of His Divine Grace A.C. Bhaktivedanta Swami Prabhupada at the first ISKCON center in New York City. He was initiated by Shrila Prabhupada in Santa Fe in 1968, receiving the name Patita Pavana Dasa Brahmachary. Later, Shrila Prabhupada changed his name to Patita Uddharana—which he said meant practically the same thing—and he continued to call Patit by either name. In India, his name somehow became shortened to Pavan, a name of the wind god.

After initiation, he hitchhiked to Los Angeles, where ISKCON was establishing its world headquarters. Shrila Prabhupada sent him to New York to learn bookbinding for the ISKCON Press. Patita went on to set up the ISKCON Press book bindery in Boston in 1969, printing thousands of copies of *Back to Godhead* magazines and books like *Nectar of Devotion* and *Shri Ishopanishad*.

In 1976, Patita joined the India BBT in Bombay, where he worked to collect reviews for Prabhupada's *Shrimad Bhagavatam* from India's leading scholars. His efforts were successful, with numerous scholars giving positive reviews that were used to promote Prabhupada's books in university libraries across India. During this time, he visited holy places, deepening his devotion.

In the 1980s and 90s, he lived in San Francisco, doing freelance writing for motorcycle magazines, where he introduced *Bhagavad-gita* to many writers. Since 2006, he has lived in Southwest Bulgaria with his wife, Abhaya Mudra Dasi, and their daughters, Yamini (22) and Jaya Radhe (18). Together, they built the Jyotir Dham Ashram in the Rila Mountains, where they engage in publishing Krishna-conscious literature and serve 5,000 clients through Mithuna Twiins Astrological Services. Their main Deities are Shri Radha-Dharmeshwara and Shri Radhika-Brij Behari ji, who manifested at their ashram by their divine will.

www.ingramcontent.com/pod-product-compliance
Lightning Source LLC
Chambersburg PA
CBHW022106040426
42451CB00007B/140